TEDTALKS

2017

Keynote

PRE-INTERMEDIATE
Student's Book

NGL.Cengage.com/Keynote

PASSWORD   keynoteStdt#

NATIONAL
GEOGRAPHIC
LEARNING

David Bohlke
with Stephanie Parker

Australia · Brazil · Mexico · Singapore · United Kingdom · United States

Contents

PRONUNCIATION	READING	LISTENING	SPEAKING	WRITING
Types of animals Intonation in questions	How the vulture became the victim	Moving people to action Listening skill: Listening for gist	Talking about endangered animals Protecting species Communication skill: Presenting arguments	An endangered species
Pausing with lists Weak forms (1): *be going to*	A passion for genealogy	My family history Listening skill: Listening for contractions and possessives	Talking about family My family Communication skill: Checking information	Inviting people to a family reunion
Word stress Sentence stress	Top picks	Interview with an author Listening skill: Taking notes while listening	Talking about books Can you guess? Communication skill: Asking for opinions	Writing a book review
/ŋ/ Stress with quantifiers	Music and the brain	A traditional singer Listening skill: Understanding accents	Talking about music Discussing musical preferences Communication skill: Describing music	Describing a favourite song
Sound and spelling Word linking	Chicago's much-loved flag	A designer's advice Listening skill: Listening for changes in topic	Talking about design Describing a coat of arms Communication skill: Talking about meaning	Describing your country's flag
that Giving emphasis	Drawing your own success	My inspiration Listening skill: Listening for expressions of uncertainty	Talking about an inspirational person Getting advice Communication skill: Finding out what someone knows	Describing an inspiring person

PRONUNCIATION	READING	LISTENING	SPEAKING	WRITING
Intonation in questions with options *will*	Leather from a lab	Sustainable chef Listening skill: Identifying main ideas in fast speech	Talking about ethical choices Predicting future habits Communication skill: Acknowledging a point	Predicting the future of food
Showing enthusiasm Stress in phrasal verbs	Having a say about your city	Living abroad Listening skill: Listening for time expressions	Talking about where you live Talking about places to go Communication skill: Giving examples	Describing a change for the better
Linking with /w/ and /j/ Intonation with conditional sentences	Giving on the go	My fundraising adventure Listening skill: Understanding directions	Talking about good causes Planning an event Communication skill: Explaining reasons	Describing a charity
Word stress with three-syllable words Pausing with adverbs of attitude	The power of the mind	The power of visualization Listening skill: Listening for instructions	Talking about a game A logic puzzle Communication skill: Explaining the uses of something	Writing a proposal
/ðə/ and /ði:/ Weak forms (2): *have*	The miracle of pollen	My experiences in nature Listening skill: Noticing auxiliary verbs	Talking about nature Experiences in nature Communication skill: Asking for more details	Writing a journal entry
Numbers and dates Irregular past participles	The dinosaur hunter	An amazing find Listening skill: Listening for numbers and dates	Talking about a discovery Discovery quiz Communication skill: Explaining possibilities	Reporting the news

TED Talk transcripts   166

Featured TED Talks

Unit 1
Why I love vultures
Munir Virani

Unit 2
The world's largest family reunion
A. J. Jacobs

Unit 3
My year reading a book from every country
Ann Morgan

Unit 4
Why I take the piano on the road … and in the air
Daria van den Bercken

Unit 6
How a boy became an artist
Jarrett J. Krosoczka

Unit 5
The worst-designed thing you've never noticed
Roman Mars

What is **TED** ?

TED has a simple goal: to spread great ideas. Every year, hundreds of presenters share ideas at TED events around the world. Millions of people watch TED Talks online. The talks inspire many people to change their attitudes and their lives.

SPREADING IDEAS WORLDWIDE

Over **17,000**
TEDx events in more than
130 countries

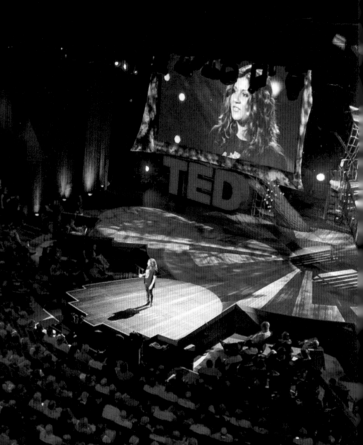

Over **2,300**
TEDTALKS available on TED.com

TEDTALKS
translated into
113 languages

Over
3,800,000,000
views of **TED**TALKS across all platforms

1 Conservation

Wooden posts support ancient
trees in Kenroku-en Garden, Japan

WARM UP

Look at the photo and read the caption. Discuss
the questions.

1 Do you think it's important to conserve old trees?

2 What else should we work hard to conserve?

3 What worries do you have for the natural world?

In this unit you:

- talk about animals
- describe events happening in
  the present
- watch a TED Talk by
  MUNIR VIRANI about the
  dangers facing vultures

A critically endangered Indochinese box turtle, photographed by Joel Sartore as part of his Photo Ark project

1.1 Animals in danger

VOCABULARY Types of animals

1 Read the paragraph about Joel Sartore's Photo Ark project. Complete the table headings with the words in **bold**.

Joel Sartore's Photo Ark project started with endangered amphibians. Sartore wanted to do something to show these species to the world before they were gone forever. Soon, Sartore heard about other animals in trouble – **mammals, reptiles, birds, fish, insects**. Now, he photographs anything that will stay still long enough for him to take a photo.

Amphibians					
frogs toads	turtles crocodiles	butterflies ants	owls flamingos	sharks tuna	tigers pandas

Pronunciation Types of animals

2 ▶ **1.1** Listen and check your answers to Exercise 1. Then listen again and repeat.

3 Work in pairs. Add one more animal to each category in the table.

4 What animals do you know that are endangered? Discuss with a partner.

I think most species of tigers are endangered.

Yeah, I think you're right.

LISTENING Moving people to action

> **Listening for gist**
> When you listen to something for the first time, just focus on the speaker's overall message. Listen again for more details.

5 ▶ **1.2** Listen to photographer Joel Sartore talking about the Photo Ark. What does he mean when he talks about 'moving people to action?'

6 ▶ **1.2** Listen again. Complete the sentences with the words you hear.

    1 'My goal is to get people to wake up and say "Whoa! That's _____!"'

    2 'I shoot _____ pictures a year, minimum.'

    3 'Maybe _____ are keepers.'

Photographer Joel Sartore

7 What might be some threats that lemurs face? Discuss with a partner.

SPEAKING Talking about endangered animals

8 ▶ **1.3** Listen to the conversation. What is the biggest danger to the Sumatran elephant?

    A: Hey! Check out these elephants.

    B: Cool! Are they African elephants?

    A: No, they're Sumatran elephants. Oh, how **awful**. It says here that they are facing extinction.   **terrible / sad**

    B: That's terrible. Does it say why?

    A: Um … **it's mostly** because people are cutting down the rainforest. But another reason is that people illegally hunt and kill them.   **it's mainly / the main reason is**

    B: How many **are there** in the wild?   **remain / still live**

    A: Let's see … between 2,400 and 2,800.

    B: They're such beautiful animals. I really hope people can find a way to **save** them.   **help / protect**

9 Practise the conversation with a partner. Practise again using the words on the right.

10 Work in pairs and make notes about an endangered animal. Join another pair and share your information.

Animal	Where do they live?	Why are they endangered?

Mountain gorillas live in Africa.

They're endangered because they're losing their habitat.

1.2 How we're helping

RISKS OF EXTINCTION

Many animals are facing threats to their survival. The International Union for Conservation of Nature uses a scale to track the conservation status of the world's animal species.

| Least concern | Near threatened | Vulnerable | Endangered | Critically endangered | Extinct |

Reindeer have a healthy population of around 3.8 million.

Polar bears are vulnerable due to climate change. Only around 20,000 remain.

Sumatran orangutans are in great danger of extinction due to habitat loss. Only 7,500 remain.

West African black rhinos were declared extinct in 2011. The main cause was poaching.

GRAMMAR Present simple and present continuous

1 ▶ 1.4 Look at the infographic. Why do you think reindeer populations are healthy?

2 ▶ 1.5 Listen to an expert talking about three species of fish. Write the conservation status of each one.

   1 barracuda: _____

   2 bigeye tuna: _____

   3 silver trout: _____

3 Read the sentences in the Grammar box. Answer the questions (a–d).

PRESENT SIMPLE AND PRESENT CONTINUOUS

1 The barracuda **is doing** pretty well and **has** a healthy population.
2 The bigeye tuna **is not doing** so well.
3 This fish often **spends** all day deep under the water.
4 These things **are threatening** the survival of the species.

a In sentence 1, which verb describes something happening now or around now?

b In sentence 1, which verb describes a fact or permanent situation?

c Which tense do we use to describe a regular event?

d How do we form the present continuous?

Check your answers on page 137 and do Exercises 1–2.

4 Choose the correct options to complete the text.

Many people are worried that the number of fish in the sea ¹*declines / is declining* but an organization called Blue Ventures ²*takes / is taking* action. They ³*is / are* working with the local community in different parts of the world to change this situation. They ⁴*also run / are also running* regular trips for young people to come and help. At the moment, Dominic ⁵*takes part / is taking part* in their project in Madagascar. He ⁶*stays / is staying* in a fishing village and every morning he and his group ⁷*go / are going* diving. He says they ⁸*are having / have* a good time, but they ⁹*don't / aren't* diving just for fun. Today, for example, he ¹⁰*collects / is collecting* data about the coral reef.

LANGUAGE FOCUS Describing events in the present

5 ▶ **1.6** Study the examples in the Language focus box.

DESCRIBING EVENTS IN THE PRESENT

To talk about regular events, facts and permanent situations

Every year, the Arctic **freezes** and **melts**.
Polar bears **live** in the Arctic.
Polar bears **hunt** seals.

Does a vulnerable species **have** any living individuals?
Yes, it **does**.
Does an extinct species **have** any living individuals?
No, it **doesn't**.

To talk about events happening now, around now or that are changing

Our planet's temperature **is rising**.
Polar bears **are** now **losing** their hunting grounds.
These days, polar bear numbers **are declining**.

Is the world's climate **changing**?
Yes, it **is**.
Is the Earth's temperature **falling**?
No, it **isn't**.
Why **are** polar bear numbers **decreasing**?
Because it's harder for them to hunt seals.

For more information and practice, go to page 138.

6 Match the questions with the responses (a–f).

   1 Do orangutans live in Southeast Asia?
   2 Where do they spend most of their time?
   3 Are their numbers declining?
   4 Why are the numbers dropping?
   5 What are people doing to protect them?
   6 Does poaching threaten them, too?

   a Yes, it does.
   b Yes, they do.
   c They're trying to conserve the forests.
   d They usually live in trees.
   e It's mainly because they're losing their habitat.
   f Yes, they are.

Pronunciation Intonation in questions

7a ▶ **1.7** Listen to the questions from Exercise 6. Which questions go up at the end (↑) and which go down (↓)?

7b ▶ **1.7** Listen again and repeat. Then complete the sentence.

   Wh- questions usually go *up / down* at the end and yes/no questions usually go *up / down*.

8 ▶ **1.8** Complete the text with the present simple or present continuous form of the verbs. Listen and check your answers.

In this photo, young green sea turtles
1_____ (make) their long and dangerous journey to the sea. Every year, the females
2_____ (lay) thousands of eggs on Florida's beaches, but many young turtles
3_____ (not become) adults because of egg hunting. Slowly, however, the situation
4_____ (change) because organizations, such as the WWF, 5_____ (help) to protect the nesting sites. Now, thanks to new laws, the numbers of green sea turtles
6_____ (not decrease) anymore and, in fact, the population 7_____ (rise). As a result, the US Fish and Wildlife Service
8_____ (think about) changing the turtle's status from endangered to threatened. In the right conditions, the green sea turtle
9_____ (live) for up to 80 years.

SPEAKING Protecting species

9 Work in pairs. What do you know about these two animal species – Bengal tigers and kiwis?

10 You are going to learn about these species. Student A: Turn to page 155. Student B: Turn to page 156.

1.3 Stop before it's too late

READING How the vulture became the victim

1 ▶ 1.9 Work in pairs. Why do you think vultures might be in danger? Read the article and check your ideas.

Understanding gist

2 According to the article, which of these best describes vultures?

   a birds that spread diseases   **c** the African lion's best friend

   b endangered birds that need our help   **d** the strangest of all bird species

Understanding main ideas

3 Match the paragraph with the main question it answers. One question is extra.

   1 Paragraph 1

   2 Paragraph 2

   3 Paragraph 3

   4 Paragraph 4

   a Why are vulture numbers in Africa declining?

   b Why did vulture populations decline in India?

   c Why is it important to protect Africa's vultures?

   d What will happen to India's vultures in the future?

   e What happened to India's vultures in the 1990s?

Understanding cause and effect

4 Why have vulture numbers declined? Use the sentences (a–f) to complete the summary.

   a A farmer places poison inside a cow's dead body.

   b People give a drug to sick cows.

   c Vultures eventually die because of diclofenac poisoning.

   d Both lions and vultures feed on the cow and they die from poisoning.

   e A lion attacks and kills a cow, so the herder decides to kill the lion.

   f Vultures start to become ill after they feed on a cow treated with medicine.

India: _____ → _____ → _____   **Africa:** _____ → _____ → _____

Understanding vocabulary

5 Match each **bold** word from the article with its definition.

   1 treat   **a** the group of people who control a country

   2 ban   **b** usual; happening often

   3 common   **c** to stop people from doing something

   4 community   **d** a group of people who live in the same area

   5 government   **e** to try to make a sick person or animal well again

6 Discuss the questions with a partner.

   1 What might be some ways to protect the vultures in Africa?

   2 What are some other ways farmers could protect their cows instead of using poison?

Without protection, many believe
vultures could soon be extinct

HOW THE VULTURE
BECAME THE VICTIM

1 In the early 1990s, something began to happen to India's vultures. Once, tens of millions of these birds filled the skies. Then, suddenly, they began to die out, victims of an unknown killer.
5 In less than a decade, the three most common Indian vulture species declined by more than 95 per cent. The Oriental white-backed vulture population – once the most common large [1]bird of prey in the world – fell by an incredible 99.9
10 per cent. It was one of the fastest population decreases of any bird species in history.

2 Scientists eventually found the cause of the decline was a pain-killing drug called diclofenac, which was used to **treat** sick livestock. Although
15 safe for cows, it kills vultures. Any vulture feeding on the [2]flesh of a cow treated with diclofenac soon becomes ill. Millions of vultures died as a result. To stop the decline, India's **government banned** the drug's use on animals in 2006.
20 Today, the country's vulture decline is slowing.

3 Conservationists are now worried something similar may be happening in Africa. The continent has already lost one of its eleven vulture species, and seven others are endangered. As with India, a major threat is poisoning. In rural 25 **communities**, it is **common** for [3]herders to lose cows and other livestock to [4]predators. When a lion attacks and kills a cow, the farmers often put poison in the cow's [5]carcass. This kills the lion when it returns to feed. However, vultures 30 also die from the poison when they feed off a poisoned carcass. Researchers believe this may be the cause of over 60 per cent of vulture deaths across Africa.

4 Hopefully, Africa can learn from India's 35 recent successes. Vultures may not be cute, say conservationists, but they are one of nature's most important [6]scavengers. Without protection, Africa's vultures may be extinct within the next 50 to 100 years. 40

---

[1] **bird of prey (n)** a bird that eats other animals
[2] **flesh (n)** the soft part of the body between the bones and skin
[3] **herder (n)** someone who looks after a group of animals

[4] **predator (n)** an animal that kills and eats other animals
[5] **carcass (n)** the body of a dead animal
[6] **scavenger (n)** an animal that eats dead animals or plants

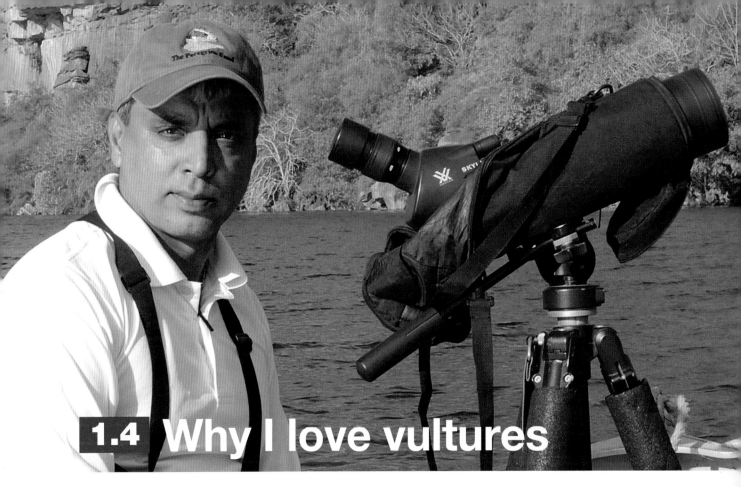

1.4 Why I love vultures

TEDTALKS

1 Read the paragraph. Match each **bold** word with its meaning (1–4). You will hear these words in the TED Talk.

> Biologist **MUNIR VIRANI** does not want people to think of vultures as **greedy** or ugly **creatures**. Instead, he wants people to understand the **ecological** services they provide. His idea worth spreading is that vultures are **vital** to the environment and to human health, and deserve to be protected.

1 extremely important: _____

2 animals of any type: _____

3 environmental: _____

4 wanting more than needed: _____

2 ▶ 1.10 Watch Part 1 of the TED Talk. Complete the notes.

Generally viewed negatively by society	Two types	Importance of vultures
• Darwin described turkey vultures as 'disgusting birds'. • Disney has often portrayed vultures as [1]_____ characters.	• New World vultures: mainly found in [2]_____ • Old World vultures: [3]_____ out of 16 species are at high risk of extinction	• clean up animal carcasses and help control the spread of [4]_____

3 ▶ 1.11 Watch Part 2 of the TED Talk. Circle the correct options to complete the sentences.

1 People are doing research to find out *where vultures go / what vultures eat*.

2 Munir Virani says that saving vultures is a(n) *local / international* problem.

3 Virani says we can all help by *visiting zoos to learn / educating people* about vultures.

4 Darwin changed his mind about vultures when he watched them *fly / clean up a carcass*.

CRITICAL THINKING

4 Has your opinion of vultures changed after watching Munir Virani's TED Talk? If so, what did he do or say to change your opinion? Discuss with a partner.

VOCABULARY IN CONTEXT

5 ▶ **1.12** Watch the clips from the TED Talk. Choose the correct meaning of the words.

6 Work in pairs. Discuss the questions.

1 Are you someone who changes your mind a lot, or do you find it easy to make decisions?

2 How do you show your friends and family that you appreciate them?

PRESENTATION SKILLS Signposting with questions

TIPS One useful way to organize a presentation is to begin each section by asking the audience a question. This helps the audience know exactly what you are going to talk about.

7 ▶ **1.13** Watch the clip. Complete the question Munir Virani asks near the start of his presentation.

'First of all, _____ such a bad press?'

8 ▶ **1.14** Match the questions Munir Virani asks with the responses he gives. Watch and check your answers.

1 So why are vultures important?

2 So what is the problem with vultures?

3 So what's being done?

4 How can you help?

a You can become active, make noise.

b First of all, they provide vital ecological services.

c Well, we're conducting research on these birds.

d We have eight species of vultures that occur in Kenya, of which six are highly threatened with extinction.

9 Imagine you are going to give a presentation on pandas. Write three key points about them. Then exchange notes with a partner. Write a signposting question for each key point.

Key points

1 _____ .

2 _____ .

3 _____ .

Questions

_____ ?

_____ ?

_____ ?

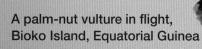

A palm-nut vulture in flight, Bioko Island, Equatorial Guinea

1.5 Which to save?

COMMUNICATE A group decision

1 Work in pairs. Match these endangered species with the photos.

| bluefin tuna | Indian python | Frégate island beetle | marine iguana |

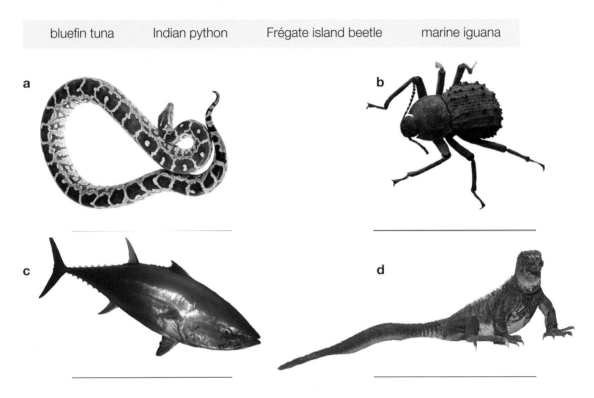

a

b

c

d

2 Work in groups of four. You are members of an organization that raises money to protect endangered species. Student A: Turn to page 155. Student B: Turn to page 156. Student C: Turn to page 158. Student D: Turn to page 160. Read the information and make notes about your animal.

3 Your organization only has enough money to help save one animal. Take turns presenting the information about your animal to your group. Then, work together to choose the one animal you are going to save.

PRESENTING ARGUMENTS

For one thing ...   Something else to consider is ...   The most important thing is ...

4 Compare your group's decision with others in the class. Which animal was most popular? Why do you think this was the case?

WRITING An endangered species

5 Write about an animal you think needs protection.

An animal that needs our protection is the polar bear. Rising sea levels are threatening its survival. We have a responsibility to save polar bears because humans cause climate change.

2 Family connections

A grandfather and grandson ride a bike together in Provence, France

WARM UP

Look at the photo and read the caption. Discuss the questions.

1 Can you describe the relationship you see in the photo?

2 How important is the grandparent–grandchild relationship?

3 Who do you have a good connection with in your extended family?

In this unit you:

- talk about family
- describe future plans
- watch a TED Talk by **A.J. JACOBS** about how we are all connected

A family comes together
at a Christmas party

2.1 Family ties

VOCABULARY Extended family

1 ▶ 2.1 Look at the family tree. Complete the sentences using the words in the box. Listen and check your answers.

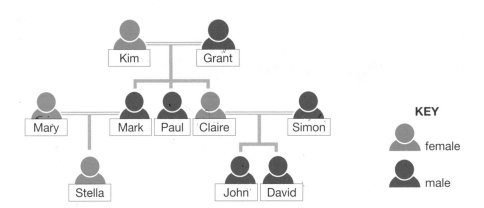

KEY

👤 female

👤 male

| brother-in-law | cousin | grandchild | grandfather |
| mother-in-law | nephew | niece | son-in-law |

1 Kim is Mary's _____ .

2 Stella is John's _____ .

3 Grant is John's _____ .

4 Simon is Kim's _____ .

5 John is Grant's _____ .

6 Simon is Paul's _____ .

7 Stella is Claire's _____ .

8 David is Mark's _____ .

2 Work in pairs. Describe a connection to someone in your family. Your partner should name the relationship.

Joanna is my mum's sister.

Is she your aunt?

LISTENING My family history

> **Listening for contractions and possessives**
> When we hear 's after a noun or a person's name, it might be a contraction of *is* or a possessive form.
>
> | **Contraction of *is*:** | **Possessive form:** |
> |---|---|
> | John's 21 years old. | John's cousin is 30 years old. |

3 ▶ **2.2** Listen to Ken Lejtenyi talking about his family history. Circle the countries that he mentions.

Canada	England	France	Hungary
Italy	Romania	Scotland	Singapore

4 ▶ **2.2** Listen again. Complete the sentences.

1 Ken's mother's parents moved to Canada from _____.

2 His mother was born in _____.

3 His father's parents met in _____.

4 His father grew up in _____.

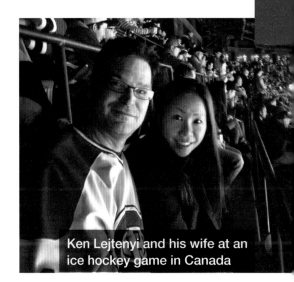

Ken Lejtenyi and his wife at an ice hockey game in Canada

Pronunciation Pausing with lists

5 ▶ **2.3** Listen. Notice how the speaker pauses after each item in the list. Practise saying the sentences.

1 So my mother, aunts and uncle were born in London.

2 While he was there, he met, fell in love with and eventually married a local girl.

SPEAKING Talking about family

6 ▶ **2.4** Listen to the conversation. Where are they going to hold the family reunion? Why?

A: What are you doing for the Lunar New Year?

B: Not much. **Do you have any plans**?   **What are you doing / What are you up to**

A: I'm going to spend it with my family. Every year, we have a family **reunion**.   **get-together / party**

B: That sounds fun. Do you have a big family?

A: Yeah. My mum has seven siblings, so I have more than twenty cousins.

B: Wow! Are they all coming to your **place**?   **house / apartment**

A: Oh, no. We're going to a restaurant. Our house is **much** too small.   **way / far**

B: Well, have a good time.

7 Practise the conversation with a partner. Practise again using the words on the right.

8 How many people are in your immediate family? How many are in your extended family? Tell a partner.

There are five people in my immediate family – my parents, my two sisters and me.

2.2 Generations

FAMILY RECORDS

The most generations alive in a single family has been seven. At 109, Augusta Bunge from the United States was the youngest living great-great-great-great-grandparent.

The highest number of children born to one mother is 69. The wife of Feodor Vassilyev from Russia (whose name is unknown) had 16 pairs of twins, seven sets of triplets and four sets of quadruplets.

HAPPY BIRTHDAY

There is only one example of a family having five single children with the same birthday. Catherine (1952), Carol (1953), Charles (1956), Claudia (1961) and Cecilia Cummins (1966) were all born on 20th February.

GRAMMAR Future plans

1 ▷ 2.5 Look at the infographic. Which record do you find the most amazing?

2 ▷ 2.6 Listen to someone talking about who she's going to meet this weekend. Circle the relationships.

   1 Chris is her *first / second* cousin.

   2 Emily is Chris's *niece / daughter*.

3 Read the sentences in the Grammar box. Choose the correct options to complete a–d.

FUTURE PLANS

1 I'm going to see my aunt during the holidays.

2 I'm meeting my aunt on Friday.

a Sentence *1 / 2* uses *to be* + *going to* + infinitive.

b Sentence *1 / 2* uses the present continuous.

c Sentence *1 / 2* means I plan or intend to see my aunt.

d Sentence *1 / 2* means I have a definite plan or arrangement to see my aunt.

Check your answers on page 138 and do Exercises 1–2.

4 ▷ 2.6 Complete the sentences from the conversation in Exercise 2. Listen again to check your answers.

   1 'Are you _____ anything interesting this weekend?'

   2 'I'm going to _____ my second cousin, Chris.'

   3 'He's _____ his daughter Emily, too.'

   4 'I'm going to _____ Chris to help me find out more about the family.'

   5 'Where are you _____ them?'

5 ▷ 2.7 Read the paragraph. Find and correct four mistakes. Listen and check your answers.

After I finish university, I going to take a year out. I think I need a break before I start working. I'm going to travel around South America with my best friend, Maki. We're meet this weekend to work out our plans. We're definitely going to start in Argentina, but we don't know where we're go after that yet. We don't have very much money so we're mainly going stay in hostels. I can't wait. It's going to be a great adventure.

LANGUAGE FOCUS Talking about future plans and arrangements

6 ▶ **2.8** Study the examples in the Language focus box.

TALKING ABOUT FUTURE PLANS AND ARRANGEMENTS

Talking about plans and intentions

I'm **going to see** my nephew this weekend.
I'm **not going to stay** for very long.

Are you **going to meet** your cousins?
Yes, I **am**. / No, I'm **not**.
What are you **going to do** afterwards?
I'm **going to visit** a few old friends.

Talking about definite plans or arrangements

I'm **leaving** for the reunion on Thursday.
I'm **not leaving** on Friday.

Are you **going** alone?
Yes, I **am**. / No, I'm **not**.
When are you **coming** back?
I'm **coming** back on Sunday.

For more information and practice, go to page 139.

7 Put the words in the correct order to make questions. Then ask and answer them with a partner.

1 this weekend / seeing / are / you / your grandparents

_____?

2 is going / which family member / to visit you / next

_____?

3 with your family / spending / you / are / your next holiday

_____?

4 you / anyone in your family / speaking to / are / this evening

_____?

Pronunciation Weak forms (1): *be going to*

8a ▶ **2.9** Listen. Notice how *are* becomes /ə/ and *to* becomes /tə/ in these sentences.

1 Where **are** you going **to** be this weekend?

2 What **are** you going **to** do?

3 Who **are** you going **to** see?

8b Work in pairs. Practise asking and answering the questions.

9 ▶ **2.10** Complete the conversation with *going to* or the present continuous form of the verb. Listen and check your answers.

A: OK, so it's all arranged. We
¹_____ (celebrate) my parents'
60th wedding anniversary on 25th August.

B: Great. Where ²_____
(you / have) the celebrations?

A: We ³_____ (all / meet) at a
hotel in Wales.

B: ⁴_____ (your sister and
brother-in-law / come)?

A: Yes, of course. But they ⁵_____
(not / arrive) until the night before the party.

B: ⁶_____ (you / see) your cousin
while you're in Wales?

A: No, I don't think so. I ⁷_____
(not / visit) that part of the country.

B: What do you think ⁸_____
(your parents / do) after the party is over?

A: I think they ⁹_____ (have) a
nice quiet holiday without the family!

SPEAKING My family

10 Find a different person who answers *yes* to
each question. For each *yes* answer, ask a
follow-up question. Take notes.

Find someone who ...

- is going to call someone in their family today.
- is going on a family holiday soon.
- has a niece or a nephew.
- is going to a family wedding this year.
- has three or more brothers and sisters.

Have you got a niece or nephew?

Yes, I have. I've got two nieces.

11 Share the most interesting information with the
class.

2.3 One big happy family

READING A passion for genealogy

1 Work in pairs. Think of some reasons why people might search for information on their family history. Discuss your ideas. Then scan the article to see if your ideas are mentioned.

Understanding purpose

2 ▶ 2.11 Read the article. What is its main purpose?

   a to explain the history of genealogy

   b to explain why people are interested in genealogy

Understanding main ideas

3 Match each paragraph with its main idea.

   1 Paragraph 1   **a** People search for their ancestors for a variety of reasons.

   2 Paragraph 2   **b** Genealogy could help solve problems in the world.

   3 Paragraph 3   **c** Genealogy is very popular on the Internet.

   4 Paragraph 4   **d** Genealogy is not new, but the Internet is changing it.

Understanding details

4 Answer the questions. Circle the correct option.

   1 What proof does the article give that genealogy is popular on the Internet?

      a   the number of Internet searches   b   statistics from an ancestry website

   2 Why are some people interested in genealogy?

      a   to see if an ancestor had a medical condition   b   to find lost family members

   3 What does the quotation from Helen Keller mean?

      a   Everyone is connected to people from different backgrounds.

      b   People often use genealogy to show a connection to rich people.

   4 Why did A. J. Jacobs become interested in genealogy?

      a   He found out he was related to a famous person.

      b   A distant relative contacted him.

Understanding vocabulary

5 Match each **bold** word from the article with its definition.

   1 wealth   **a** legally made part of a family you were not born into

   2 ancestors   **b** a feeling of wanting to find out about something

   3 adopted   **c** a feeling of wanting something

   4 curiosity   **d** people in your family from past times

   5 desire   **e** a large amount of money

6 To find out more about your family history, who would you talk to first? What questions would you ask? Discuss with a partner.

A PASSION FOR GENEALOGY

1 Genealogy, the study of family history, is certainly nothing new. Family trees have been used for thousands of years, often to demonstrate our rights to **wealth** and power. But the rise of
5 the Internet has made it much more popular than ever before.

2 According to some sources, genealogy is now one of the most popular topics on the Internet. Modern genealogists have a huge amount of
10 information available online, and are able to connect with people from all around the world. One popular ancestry website provides access to approximately sixteen billion historical records. Its two million [1]subscribers have added 200 million
15 photographs, documents and stories to connect with 70 million family trees.

3 But what makes us want to know about our **ancestors**? Some people may have specific reasons. Getting to know your family tree may help you reconnect with lost relatives. **Adopted** children 20 can find out more about their birth parents. Others may want to discover a connection to a historical figure. Perhaps the most common [2]motivation, though, is simply **curiosity** – a **desire** to better understand our place in the world. Genealogy can 25 show our connections with people from entirely different backgrounds. As [3]Helen Keller once said, 'There is no king who has not had a [4]slave among his ancestors, and no slave who has not had a king among his.' 30

4 A. J. Jacobs's interest in genealogy started when he received an email from his twelfth cousin. Since then, Jacobs has joined one of the world's biggest family trees on Geni.com, which includes more than 75 million people. Jacobs believes that 35 if we all realized that we're connected in this way, it could solve a lot of the problems in the world. As Jacobs says, 'We're not just part of the same species. We're part of the same family.'

---

[1] **subscriber (n)** someone who pays to get access to a website or to receive copies of a newspaper or magazine

[2] **motivation (n)** a reason for doing something

[3] **Helen Keller (pn)** an American writer, educator and activist who was both blind and deaf

[4] **slave (n)** a person who is the legal property of another person

2.4 The world's largest family reunion

TEDTALKS

1 Read the paragraph. Complete the definitions (1–3). You will hear these words in the TED Talk.

> Writer **A. J. JACOBS** finds genealogy **fascinating**. After receiving an email from a man who claimed to be his twelfth cousin, Jacobs began planning a huge family reunion to meet his extended family. His idea worth spreading is that studying the world's 'family tree' helps scientific progress, brings history alive and encourages us to **treat** other people better by making us realize we are **interconnected**.

    1 Something that is **fascinating** is extremely *well-known / interesting*.

    2 If you **treat** people better, you are *kinder to them / understand them more*.

    3 If people are **interconnected**, they are *biologically related / the same*.

2 ▶ **2.12** Watch Part 1 of the TED Talk. Tick (✓) the points A. J. Jacobs makes.

    a Genealogy is undergoing a revolution partly because of genetics and the Internet.

    b People can add their own information online to create and combine huge family trees.

    c Putting our personal family information online can be a dangerous thing to do.

    d Most people have famous people and historical figures in their family trees.

3 ▶ **2.13** Watch Part 2 of the TED Talk. A. J. Jacobs gives four reasons why a world family tree is a good idea. Match each idea to a supporting detail.

Main ideas	Supporting details
1 It has scientific value.	**a** We all come from the same ancestor.
2 It brings history alive.	**b** We treat family better than we treat strangers.
3 It shows we are all connected.	**c** Jacobs found out he was related to a famous person.
4 It creates a kinder world.	**d** It provides a better understanding of human migration.

4 ▶ **2.14** Watch Part 3 of the TED Talk. Complete the notes.

    Event   The biggest _____ in history

    Activities   Exhibits, _____, _____, a day of _____

    Who's invited?   _____

CRITICAL THINKING

5 A.J. Jacobs uses humour to engage his audience. Why does the audience laugh at these sentences? Which do you find funniest?

   1 Here's my cousin Gwyneth Paltrow. She has no idea I exist, but we are officially cousins. We have just seventeen links between us.

   2 Now Albert Einstein is not some dead white guy with weird hair. He's Uncle Albert.

VOCABULARY IN CONTEXT

6 ▶ 2.15 Watch the clips from the TED Talk. Choose the correct meaning of the words.

7 Work in pairs. Complete the sentences in your own words.

   1 Here's something I learned recently: it turns out that …

   2 I don't want to boast, but I'm quite good at …

PRESENTATION SKILLS Personalizing a presentation

> **TIPS**
>
> Some speakers choose to include personal information in their presentations. Including stories about yourself, or your family members, can help engage your audience and make your presentation more 'real'.

8 ▶ 2.16 Watch the clip. What does Jacobs do to personalize the presentation?

   a He talks about his uncle.
      c He tells a personal story.

   b He shows a photo of a family member.

9 ▶ 2.17 Jacobs personalizes his presentation in other ways. Match the phrases below. Watch the clips to check your answer.

   1 '[Genealogy] brings history alive.'
      a 'I have three sons, so I see how they fight.'

   2 'Now, I know there are family feuds.'
      b 'Here's my cousin Gwyneth Paltrow. She has no idea I exist, but we are officially cousins.'

   3 'So that's 75 million people connected by blood or marriage.'
      c 'I found out I'm connected to Albert Einstein, so I told my seven-year-old son that and he was totally engaged.'

10 Work in pairs. Imagine you are giving a talk on these topics. How could you use personalization?

   the cost of living   climate change   an endangered animal

A. J. Jacobs at the Global Family Reunion

I AM A COUSIN

2.5 Who's that?

COMMUNICATE Making a family tree

1 Work in a group of four. You are going to work together to draw a family tree.
Student A: Turn to page 155. Student B: Turn to page 156. Student C: Turn to page 158.
Student D: Turn to page 160.

2 Read out pieces of information and ask each other questions to find how everyone is
related to each other. Complete the family tree.

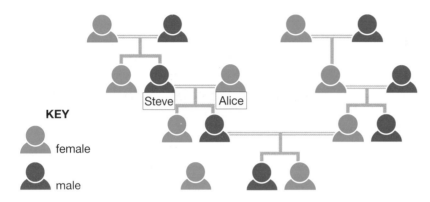

KEY

 female

male

Alice is Steve's wife.

OK. Do they have any children?

CHECKING INFORMATION

John is …, isn't he?   Are you saying that they're ….?
Let me just check something, did you say …?

WRITING Inviting people to a family reunion

3 You are organizing a family reunion. Decide when and where it's going to be.
Write a group email to your family members telling them the details.

Hi everyone!

I have great news! I'm organizing a family reunion, and you're all invited! It's going to
take place on July 22–23, so I hope you're free then. It's going to be at …

3 Global stories

Performers use giant puppets to tell a story in a shadow play, Thailand

WARM UP

Look at the photo and read the caption. Discuss the questions.

1 Are puppets a good way to tell a story? Why? / Why not?

2 Have you ever seen a puppet show? What kind of puppets?

3 What other different ways can you think of to tell a story?

In this unit you:

- talk about stories
- define people, things and places
- watch a TED Talk by **ANN MORGAN** about her unusual reading project

The Abbey Library of Saint Gallen, Switzerland, is one of the oldest libraries in the world

3.1 It's a great story

VOCABULARY Describing stories

1 Match each adjective with its definition.

1 charming	**a** showing how things are in real life
2 powerful	**b** having a strong effect on people's feelings or opinions
3 realistic	**c** very pleasing and enjoyable
4 mysterious	**a** difficult to understand because it has a lot of different parts
5 surprising	**b** full of secrets
6 complicated	**c** unusual and unexpected
7 moving	**a** making you feel strong emotions of sadness or sympathy
8 dramatic	**b** very scary
9 terrifying	**c** exciting and full of action

Pronunciation Word stress

2 ▷ **3.1** Look at the adjectives in Exercise 1. Underline where you think the stress goes on each word. Listen and check. Then listen again and repeat.

3 Work in pairs. Can you think of books you could describe with the adjectives?

The Lord of the Rings is complicated but also very dramatic.

4 Look at these elements of a story. Then think of a book and describe it to your partner.

Characters: who the story is about

Setting: where and when the story takes place

Plot: what happens in the story

Theme: the central idea of the story

LISTENING Interview with an author

> **Taking notes while listening**
> When you listen and take notes at the same time, don't write down everything you hear. Be selective and write down only the key words and phrases.

5 ▶ **3.2** Madeleine Thien is a prize-winning author. Listen and circle **T** for true or **F** for false.

1 As a child, Thien knew she wanted to be an author.   **T**   **F**

2 Thien's first book was a novel.   **T**   **F**

3 The setting for one of her stories is Canada.   **T**   **F**

6 ▶ **3.2** Listen again and take notes on these points.

- Date first book published
- Title of book
- Number of stories
- Main theme
- Reviews?
- How many other books?

7 Do you think you'd enjoy this book? Why or why not? Discuss with a partner.

Madeleine Thien

SPEAKING Talking about books

8 ▶ **3.3** Listen to the conversation. What's the book about?

A: What are you reading?

B: Oh, it's a book called *And Then There Were None*. Do you know it?

A: No, I don't think so. What kind of book is it? Is it a novel?

B: Yes, it's a mystery. **It's about** a group of people   **It's a story about / It tells the story of**
who are stuck on an island together.

A: It sounds cool. Is it **any good**?   **worth reading / interesting**

B: Yeah, **I can't put it down**.   **it's really dramatic / it's very exciting**

A: Wow! Can I borrow it when you've finished?

B: Of course. I think you'll like it.

9 Practise the conversation with a partner. Practise again using the words on the right.

10 Work in pairs. What's your favourite book? Explain what it's about.

My favourite book is *Hyperion* by Dan Simmons. It's a science fiction story about six characters who visit the planet Hyperion.

3.2 What's it about?

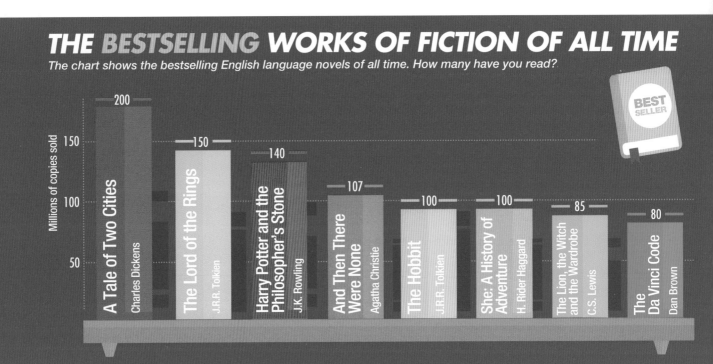

THE BESTSELLING WORKS OF FICTION OF ALL TIME

The chart shows the bestselling English language novels of all time. How many have you read?

GRAMMAR Defining relative clauses

1 ▷ 3.4 Look at the infographic. Which of these books have you read?

2 ▷ 3.5 Listen to two people talking about one of the books. Complete the sentences.

The Lion, the Witch and the Wardrobe is a ¹_____ book about four ²_____
who live in an old house. They go through a magical wardrobe and visit a place called Narnia. Narnia is
a place where ³_____ can talk.

3 ▷ 3.6 Read the sentences in the Grammar box. Choose the correct options to complete a–c.

DEFINING RELATIVE CLAUSES

Defining people

And Then There Were None is about a group of people **who** are stuck on an island.

One of the characters is a young woman **that** teaches at a girls' school.

Defining things

A Tale of Two Cities is a piece of historical fiction **that** is set in London and Paris.

The Da Vinci Code is a mystery novel **which** takes place in a 24-hour time period.

Defining places

Narnia is a magical place **where** animals can talk.

a We can use *who* and *that* with *people / things*.
b We can use *that* and *which* with *things / places*.
c We use *where* with *things / places*.

Check your answers on page 140 and do Exercises 1–2.

---

4 Match the two parts to make sentences.

1 *The Hobbit* is a fantasy adventure
2 *The Da Vinci Code* is about two people
3 The Harry Potter books are stories
4 Harry Potter is a wizard
5 *She* is set in a lost African kingdom

a where two adventurers meet a mysterious queen.
b who studies magic at school.
c who investigate a murder in Paris.
d that takes place in Middle Earth.
e that are popular with both children and adults.

5 ▶ 3.7 Find and correct four mistakes in the text. Listen and check your answers.

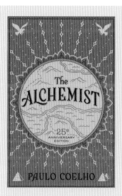

The Alchemist, by Brazilian novelist Paulo Coelho, is a story about a shepherd boy where goes on a long adventure. After many years of having the same dream, he travels to the pyramids in Egypt to look for the treasure what his dreams told him about. Along the way, he meets people who teaches him many life lessons. It's a novel who is both charming and dramatic. I would recommend this book to anyone who wants to read a powerful and moving story about becoming who you want to be.

6 Complete the sentences with *that*, *who* or *where*.

1 It's the name for a non-fiction book _____ gives you factual information.
2 He's the man _____ wrote the best-selling book in the world.
3 It's a Japanese word _____ means to buy a book and then not read it.
4 He's a famous fictional detective _____ lives in London.
5 It's the country _____ people spend the most time reading.
6 It's a story about a girl with long hair _____ falls down a hole.

Pronunciation Sentence stress

7a ▶ 3.8 Listen and check your answers to Exercise 6. Which words give the important information? Listen again and underline the words that are stressed in each sentence.

7b Work in pairs. Take turns saying the sentences in Exercise 6. Remember to stress the key words. Who or what do you think each sentence describes? Circle the correct option below. Check your answers on page 161.

1 a reference book / a comic book
2 Dickens / Cervantes
3 tsundoku / wabi sabi
4 Hercule Poirot / Sherlock Holmes
5 Australia / India
6 *Alice in Wonderland* / *Little Red Riding Hood*

8 Complete the sentences with your own ideas. Then compare with a partner.

1 I like stories that _____
_____.
2 I like authors who _____
_____.
3 I don't enjoy books that _____
_____.
4 My favourite book has a character who _____
_____.

SPEAKING Can you guess?

9 Think of a famous book or story. Write three sentences to describe it.

1 _____.
2 _____.
3 _____.

10 Work in pairs. Take turns reading your sentences. After each sentence, try to guess the name of the book or story.

This is a very famous children's book set in England.

Sorry, I don't know. Give me another clue.

It's about a boy who can fly and never grows up.

3.3 A world in books

READING Top picks

1 ▶ **3.9** Read the article quickly. Why did Ann Morgan like each book?

Understanding details

2 Read the article again. Complete the sentences with these book titles.

> Crowfall   Lake Como   The Blue Sky

1 _____ is about a group of people and the losses some of them experience.

2 _____ is about a boy and the changes that are happening in his culture.

3 _____ is about a writer who makes meaningful connections with people.

3 Complete the table.

Title	Setting	Character(s)	Theme
Lake Como			
Crowfall			
The Blue Sky			

Making inferences

4 Which reader comment do you think belongs to each book? Match.

1 *Lake Como*	**a**	'It's sad that customs from the past are no longer practised today.'
2 *Crowfall*	**b**	'It made me think a lot about my grandmother. She died last year.'
3 *The Blue Sky*	**c**	'I couldn't put it down, I was laughing so hard.'

Understanding vocabulary

5 Match each **bold** word from the article with its definition.

1 **identity**	**a**	giving information
2 **ambitious**	**b**	extremely good
3 **revealing**	**c**	the beliefs and qualities of a person
4 **glimpse**	**d**	wanting to be successful
5 **marvellous**	**e**	a quick look

6 Which book would you like to read? Why? Discuss with a partner.

TOP PICKS

Writer and blogger Ann Morgan loves to share her passion for books. Here are three books she highly recommends.

Lake Como by Srdjan Valjarević

This very funny book follows a Serbian writer named Frank who receives a ¹scholarship and moves to Italy to write. But he doesn't do any work. Instead, he spends his days chatting, watching TV and sleeping. Frank doesn't write his book, but
5 the connections he makes with the local people become more important. The book is about those connections, as well as the meaning of culture and **identity**.

Ann Morgan found it 'a great read' and says it 'has that rare gift of revealing how people can grow and learn from one another'.

Crowfall by Shanta Gokhale

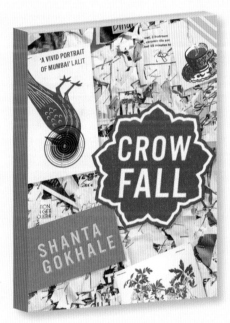

Crowfall is a big, **ambitious** book. The story follows a group of 10 characters who are just starting their careers in Mumbai, India – three painters, a musician, a journalist and a teacher. The book highlights some **revealing** things about art and music, but is mainly about loss. Throughout the story, there are several deaths that occur and a loved one goes missing. 15

Morgan called this book 'a **marvellous** read', and especially loved the author's clear, powerful language.

The Blue Sky by Galsan Tschinag

The Blue Sky is a ²coming-of-age story about a young boy
20 named Dshurukuwaa who lives in Mongolia's Altai Mountains. It's a world that is changing. All around Dshurukuwaa, the traditions of his ancestors are being lost under the pressures of modern life. In the novel, we get a fascinating **glimpse** into a way of living that is fast disappearing.

25 This was one of Morgan's favourite books. She wrote in her blog that it was 'impossible not to feel connected to and invested in this world'.

---

¹ **scholarship (n)** a sum of money given to support a student's education

² **coming-of-age story (n)** a story that focuses on a character's growth from youth to adulthood

3.4 My year reading a book from every country

TEDTALKS

1 Read the paragraph. Match each **bold** word with its meaning (1–4). You will hear these words in the TED Talk.

> **ANN MORGAN** made an **alarming** discovery several years ago when she looked at her bookshelves and saw how **narrow** her reading focus was. Her idea worth spreading is that stories from other countries and cultures have **extraordinary** power to introduce us to new values and ideas, and to show us our own **blind spots**.

1 limited: _____

2 frightening, shocking: _____

3 impressive, remarkable: _____

4 things you aren't aware of: _____

2 ▶ 3.10 Watch Part 1 of the TED Talk. Answer the questions.

1 What did Ann Morgan discover about her bookshelf?

  a Most of her books were by American or British authors.

  b Most of the books she owned were set in England.

2 What goal did Morgan set for herself?

  a She would read one book from a different country every year.

  b She would read a book from every country in a year.

3 ▶ 3.11 Watch Part 2 of the TED Talk. Number the events in the order they happened (1–5).

  a Strangers began to offer suggestions. _____

  b Morgan asked for book suggestions. _____

  c Friends and family began to offer suggestions. _____

  d Ann Morgan registered her blog. ___*1*___

  e Morgan received two books from someone in Malaysia. _____

4 ▶ 3.11 Watch Part 2 of the TED Talk again. What surprised Ann Morgan about the response to her project? Discuss with a partner.

5 ▶ **3.12** Watch Part 3 of the TED Talk. What did Ann Morgan learn from her experience? Tick (✓) the statements that she would agree with.

    a You see the world in a different way.

    b The countries that you read about begin to feel more real.

    c You can get a complete picture of a country by reading a book.

    d Books have the power to connect people.

CRITICAL THINKING

6 Reading is one way to open your eyes to other cultures. Can you think of other ways? How have *you* learned about other countries?

VOCABULARY IN CONTEXT

7 ▶ **3.13** Watch the clips from the TED Talk. Choose the correct meaning of the words.

8 Work in pairs. Discuss the questions.

    1 How do most of your friends get in touch with you? How do you prefer to communicate with people?

    2 Can you think of something that is changing little by little where you live?

PRESENTATION SKILLS Closing a presentation

TIPS

One way to close a presentation is to ask the audience to join you in supporting or acting on something. Here are other ways to end a presentation.

Summarize your main points.
Use an inspiring quotation.
Add a personal story.
Show a powerful visual.

Return to the idea you opened your presentation with.
Describe your hope for the future.

9 ▶ **3.14** Watch part of Ann Morgan's TED Talk. How does she end her presentation?

    a She shows a powerful visual.

    b She uses a quotation from an author.

    c She talks about her hopes for the future.

10 ▶ **3.15** Now watch TED speaker Munir Virani. Tick (✓) the ways he closes his presentation.

    a He shows powerful visuals.   **c** He shares a personal story.

    b He gives a call to action.   **d** He asks the audience a question.

11 Work in a group. Whose closing do you think is more effective — Virani's or Morgan's? Why?

3.5 A good read

COMMUNICATE A book recommendation

1 Work in a group. Brainstorm a list of books from your country. Include books from a variety of genres, such as novels, autobiographies, children's stories and fiction.

2 Imagine that Ann Morgan asked you for a suggestion on a book to read from your country. Agree on one book and list two reasons why it's a good choice.

> Book title:
>
> Author:
>
> Genre:
>
> What it's about:
>
> Reason 1:
>
> Reason 2:

Which book do you think we should recommend?

I think we should suggest …

ASKING FOR OPINIONS

Which do you think …?   In your opinion, what's …?   What do you feel is …?

3 Take turns presenting your book suggestions. Answer any questions from the class.

WRITING Writing a book review

4 Write a short review of a book you have read. Include the title, author and information about the setting, characters and plot.

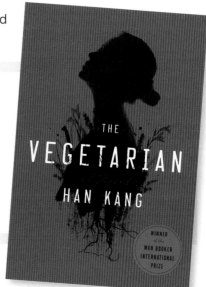

A strange but interesting story   ★★★★

I recently read *The Vegetarian* by Korean writer Han Kang. The story takes place in South Korea. The main characters are Yeong-hye and her husband, Mr Cheong. Yeong-hye doesn't want to follow society's rules. After she has a frightening dream, she decides to become a vegetarian.

5 Work in a group. Read each other's reviews. In your opinion, which book sounds the most interesting? Why?

Presentation 1 | UNITS 1–3

MODEL PRESENTATION

1 Complete the transcript of the presentation using these words.

cousin	endangered	facing	going to	help
reptile	that	travelling	where	work

I'd like to talk to you about an amazing ¹_____ that really needs our help – the sea turtle. Last month, I went diving off the coast of Mozambique in Africa with my ²_____, Maria. I saw so many amazing things, but the animal ³_____ I remember more than any others was this beautiful loggerhead sea turtle. My dive instructor told me how lucky I was. He said that sea turtles were ⁴_____ and seeing one wasn't so common any more. I later found out that many turtles are killed by humans for their eggs, meat, skin and shells. The turtles' habitats and the coastal areas ⁵_____ they lay their eggs are also under threat. So, how can you ⁶_____? Well, firstly, when you're ⁷_____, be careful what you buy. Ask questions if you think a souvenir might be made from a turtle shell. Secondly, support a turtle charity. There are many organizations that ⁸_____ to help save sea turtles. I'm now a member of a sea turtle charity and next month I'm ⁹_____ take part in a fundraising event. Finally, you can spread the word. Tell other people about these animals and the dangers they are ¹⁰_____.

Thank you so much.

2 ▶ **P.1** Watch the presentation and check your answers.

3 ▶ **P.1** Review the list of presentation skills from units 1–3. Which does the speaker use? Tick (✓) each skill used as you watch again.

Presentation skills: Units 1–3	
The speaker …	
• uses questions to signpost	☐
• personalizes the presentation	☐
• closes the presentation effectively	☐

4 Look at the notes the speaker made before her presentation. Did she forget to say anything?

> • Introduction: amazing reptile / sea turtle
> • Trip to Mozambique / diving
> • Dive instructor / lucky / endangered
> • Turtles killed for eggs/meat etc. / habitat threatened
> • How can you help?
> • Careful what you buy and eat when abroad
> • Support a charity / spread the word

YOUR TURN

5 You are going to plan and give a short presentation to a partner introducing an endangered animal. Use the notes above for ideas and research any other information. Make notes on a card or a small piece of paper.

6 Look at the Useful phrases box. Think about which ones you will need in your presentation.

USEFUL PHRASES

Introducing your topic	Types of animals
I'd like to tell you / talk to you about …	amphibians, birds, fish, insects, mammals, reptiles
Describing conservation status	**Signposting questions**
threatened, vulnerable, (critically) endangered, extinct	Why do they need our help? / How can you help?

Ending

Thank you so much (for listening).
Thanks for listening.

7 Work in pairs. Take turns giving your presentation using your notes. Use some of the presentation skills from units 1–3. As you listen, tick (✓) each skill your partner uses.

Presentation skills: Units 1–3	
The speaker …	
• uses questions to signpost	☐
• personalizes the presentation	☐
• closes the presentation effectively	☐

8 Give your partner some feedback on their talk. Include two things you liked, and one thing he or she can improve.

> Well done! You spoke really clearly and I loved the way you personalized the presentation. Next time, try to make more eye contact with your audience.

4 Music

Friends come together to sing in
a park in Sevastopol, Crimea

WARM UP

Look at the photo and read the caption. Discuss
the questions.

1 What do you think music means for the women in
the photo?

2 Have you had experiences of singing or playing
music in a group?

3 What role does music play in your life?

In this unit you:

- describe music
- talk about quantity
- watch a TED Talk by
  DARIA VAN DEN BERCKEN
  about her unusual
  concerts

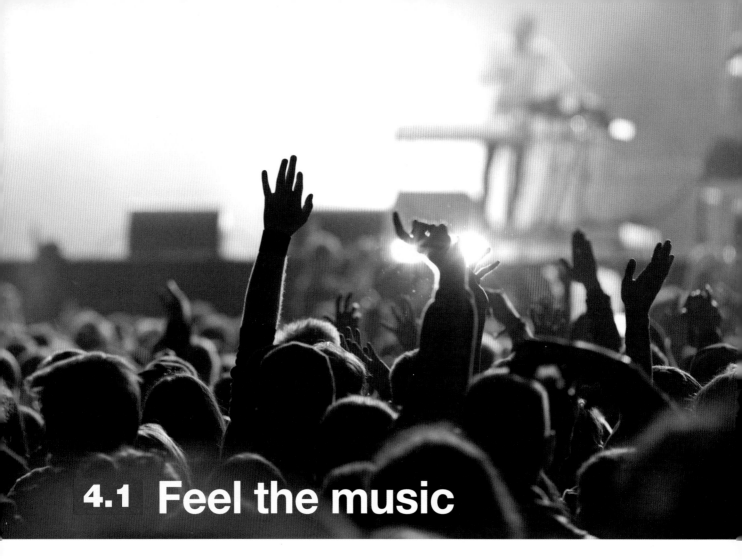

4.1 Feel the music

VOCABULARY Music

1 ▶ 4.1 Listen and number the musical genres in the order you hear them (1–6).

a classical _____

b country _____

c electronic _____

d easy listening _____

e heavy metal _____

f hip-hop _____

2 Work in pairs. Look at these words to describe music and how it makes you feel. Add the words to the correct column in the table.

depressed   cheerful   gentle   lively   loud   peaceful
relaxed   rhythmic   romantic   sleepy   soft   upbeat

Music	Feeling	Both
gentle	depressed	cheerful

3 ▶ 4.1 Listen again to the music from Exercise 1. Describe how each type sounds or makes you feel.

The easy listening music is very soft.

Yeah, it makes me feel really relaxed.

LISTENING A traditional singer

> **Understanding accents**
> At first an unfamiliar accent can be difficult to understand. Use the context to help you, and try to identify the vowel sounds that are different. You can also listen to other examples of the same accent to increase your familiarity with it.

4 ▶ **4.2** Iarla Ó Lionáird is a musician who sings in a style called *sean-nós*. Listen. Which country does sean-nós singing come from?

5 ▶ **4.2** Listen again. Circle **T** for True or **F** for False.

   1 Iarla Ó Lionáird sings in English.   **T**   **F**

   2 Some of his relatives were also singers.   **T**   **F**

   3 Ó Lionáird's teacher, Mrs McSweeney, encouraged him to sing.   **T**   **F**

   4 Ó Lionáird released his first solo album in 2014.   **T**   **F**

6 ▶ **4.3** Complete these extracts from Ó Lionáird's story. Listen and check.

   1 I remember my _____ day in school.

   2 I remember she lifted me _____ and she stood me _____ a desk.

   3 I was _____ five, and she said, 'sing'.

Iarla Ó Lionáird performing live

Pronunciation /ŋ/

7 ▶ **4.4** Listen and underline the /ŋ/ sound in these words. Then listen again and repeat.

   1 singer   **2** English   **3** language   **4** waiting   **5** award-winning

SPEAKING Talking about music

8 ▶ **4.5** Listen to the conversation. What kind of music is the man listening to?

   A: What are you listening to?

   B: Oh, it's a band called The National. Here, listen.

   A: Hey, they're pretty good. I've never heard them before.

   B: Yeah, they're not super **famous**, but they've been   **well-known / popular**
      around a while. They've made a lot of albums.

   A: This song's great. I love this kind of gentle rock.

   B: Me too. But they have a few really loud, **upbeat**   **rhythmic / lively**
      songs too. Here, listen to this one.

   A: Wow! I like it. Do you have **many of their albums**?   **much of their stuff / a lot of their music**

   B: I have them all. They're doing a **concert** here in July. I can't wait.   **gig / show**

9 Practise the conversation with a partner. Practise again using the words on the right.

10 Work in pairs. Tell each other about a band or singer that you like. Explain why.

> I really like Norah Jones. She has such a good voice.

4.2 Getting into a good rhythm

WHAT'S THE BEST MUSIC FOR ...?

STUDYING
Best music: classical or instrumental music
Examples: Mozart's sonatas or Spanish guitar
Why? It makes it easier for you to concentrate and take in new information.

GETTING TO SLEEP
Best music: soft classical music
Examples: the works of Handel and Bach
Why? It slows down brainwaves and helps you relax.

EXERCISING
Best music: electronic, hip-hop or pop songs
Examples: Lady Gaga's *Applause*
Why? It has a fast and regular rhythm.

DRIVING
Best music: pop songs with a gentle tempo
Examples: Justin Timberlake's *Cry me a river*
Why? The rhythm matches your heartbeat and keeps you calm so you drive carefully.

GRAMMAR Countable and uncountable nouns

1 ▶ **4.6** Look at the infographic. When is a good time to listen to classical music?

2 ▶ **4.7** Listen to a music expert talking about the best music to listen to while studying. Circle the types of music he recommends.

  1 songs *with* / *without* words

  2 songs you *like* / *dislike*

  3 music on *the radio* / *an album*

3 Read the sentences in the Grammar box. Choose the correct options to complete a–d.

COUNTABLE AND UNCOUNTABLE NOUNS

Many **students** listen to music when they study.

Some **research** suggests that music can help us study.

Do you listen to much classical **music?**

I keep a few jazz **CDs** in the car.

  a 'Student' and 'CD' are *countable* / *uncountable* nouns.

  b 'Research' and 'music' are *countable* / *uncountable* nouns.

  c *Countable* / *uncountable* nouns have both singular and plural forms.

  d *Countable* / *uncountable* nouns have no plural form and use a singular verb.

Check your answers on page 141 and do Exercises 1–2.

4 Are these words used with countable nouns (C), uncountable nouns (U) or both (C/U)? Put them in the correct column in the table.

any	a few	a little	a lot of
many	much	some	

C	U	C/U

Pronunciation Stress with quantifiers

5 ▶ **4.8** Listen. Notice where the stress falls in these sentence pairs. Practise saying the sentences.

  1 a I have a lot of music.

    b I have a lot.

  2 a We only have a few CDs.

    b We only have a few.

  3 a I don't listen to any jazz music.

    b I don't listen to any.

LANGUAGE FOCUS Talking about quantity

6 ▶ 4.9 Study the examples in the Language focus box.

TALKING ABOUT QUANTITY	
Countable	**Uncountable**
There were **too many** people.	There was **too much** noise.
Do you have **many songs** on your phone? I have **lots of** / **a lot of** pop songs. I don't have **many** country songs.	Do you have **much music** on your phone? I have **lots of** / **a lot of** pop music. I don't have **much** country music.
How many people were at the concert? There were **lots** / **a lot**. There were only **a few**.	**How much** traffic was there? There was **lots** / **a lot**. There was only **a little**.

For more information and practice, go to page 142.

7 Complete the sentences. Circle the correct words.

1 A: Do you know *any* / *some* of his early music? I think it's really interesting.

   B: No, I don't. Tell me *some* / *any* good songs to listen to.

2 A: Did it take *many* / *much* time to download that new song?

   B: Yeah. I think too *many* / *much* people were trying to download it at once.

3 A: *Were* / *Was* there a big crowd at the concert?

   B: Not really. There were only a *few* / *little* people.

8 ▶ 4.10 Complete the text. Circle the correct words. Listen and check your answers.

If you're a student who's struggling with too ¹*many* / *much* exams, a ²*few* / *little* classical music might just help. According to ³*many* / *much* different academic studies, classical music has ⁴*many* / *much* benefits for your brain and body that can make a difference at exam time. It's been shown that listening to classical music has an effect on how ⁵*many* / *much* new information you can learn. And if you're stressed or not getting ⁶*many* / *much* sleep, classical music can help too. It can help you relax and is also said to reduce blood pressure.

9 Correct the mistake in each sentence.

1 I love this band, but they don't do many live concert these days.

2 The performer stopped because there was too many noise coming from the crowd.

3 I was amazed by how few equipment the band had on stage.

4 After the band finished their last song, there were a lot of applause.

SPEAKING Discussing musical preferences

10 Work in pairs. Interview your partner using these questions. Then share the most interesting information you heard with the class.

What's the best music for…
- studying late at night?
- a long-distance drive?
- a party?

What do you think is the best music for a party?

4.3 It's our song

READING Music and the brain

1 ▶ 4.11 Listen to part of Johannes Brahms' Hungarian Dance No. 5. How does it make you feel? Discuss with a partner.

Understanding gist

2 ▶ 4.12 Read the article. Which two questions does the article discuss?

    a Why does music affect our emotions?   **c** When did our brains first hear music?

    b What is the happiest music to listen to?   **d** Why do different people like different music?

Understanding details

3 Circle the best answer for each question.

    1 Why was Hungarian Dance No. 5 special for Valorie Salimpoor?

        a It brought back a very happy memory.

        b It had a strong emotional effect on her.

    2 What is the main idea of Paragraph 2?

        a Researchers found a link between music and chemical activity in the brain.

        b An experiment showed that classical music usually makes people happy.

    3 What does 'templates' in Paragraph 3 refer to?

        a special tools that are used in brain scan experiments

        b patterns in the brain that relate to certain types of music

    4 The following sentence would be best placed at the end of which paragraph?

        Right then, she decided on her future career.

        a Paragraph 1   b Paragraph 2   c Paragraph 3

    5 What does 'mystery' in Paragraph 4 refer to?

        a what happens in our brains when we listen to music

        b where memory templates are stored in the brain

Understanding vocabulary

4 Complete each sentence using the correct form of the **bold** words in the article.

    1 A scientist usually has to do a lot of _____ as part of their job.

    2 Most types of food and drink contain many different _____.

    3 The earthquake _____ 7.2 on the Richter scale.

    4 I couldn't understand him because his accent was _____.

    5 When they _____ the data, they found some very surprising results.

5 What kinds of music have the greatest effect on you? Why do you think those types of music are special? Discuss with a partner.

MUSIC AND THE BRAIN

1 One day several years ago, Valorie Salimpoor went for a drive that changed her life. Salimpoor, a [1] neuroscience graduate, was struggling to decide on her career path. She felt that a drive might help

5 clear her head. When she turned on the car radio, a piece of violin music came on – Brahms' Hungarian Dance No. 5. 'Something just happened', she recalls. 'I just felt this rush of emotion ... it was so intense.' She stopped the car so she could focus

10 on the music. She wondered why it had such a powerful effect on her.

2 Salimpoor found a job working as a neuroscientist. Her **research** involved scanning the brain activity of people as they listened to

15 music. She discovered that when people listen to music they like, their brains fill with dopamine – a **chemical** linked with pleasure and motivation. In one experiment, people listened to the first 30 seconds of unfamiliar songs. In order to assess

20 how much people liked the music, the listeners were given the option of buying the full songs, using their own money. By **analysing** dopamine-related areas of the [2] participants' brains, Salimpoor was able to successfully predict which

25 songs the people would buy.

3 But why might one person like a song while another person doesn't? Salimpoor says it all depends on past musical experiences. 'Eastern, Western, jazz, heavy metal, pop – all of these have different rules they follow', she says. These 30 rules are recorded as patterns, or templates, in the brain. If the new music has a familiar template, your brain releases dopamine and **registers** a feeling of pleasure. However, if the new music has **unfamiliar** patterns, less dopamine is released. 35 This might explain why most people have a preference for a certain type of music.

4 There are questions Salimpoor is still trying to answer. For example, how does our brain make musical templates? Why do people with similar 40 backgrounds have different preferences? Her research, though, has given her a new way to think about her experience years ago. 'That day', she says, 'it all seemed like such a big mystery.' Now when she hears a piece of music she likes, she has 45 a better understanding of what's happening inside her brain.

---

[1] **neuroscience (n)** the study of the brain and nervous system

[2] **participant (n)** someone who takes part in an activity or event

4.4 Why I take the piano on the road ... and in the air

TEDTALKS

1 Read the paragraph. Complete the definitions (1–3). You will hear these words in the TED Talk.

> A few years ago, **DARIA VAN DEN BERCKEN** discovered George Handel's keyboard music. When she started to play it, she was in complete **awe**. What she experienced that day set her on a journey to share the beauty of music with others. Her idea worth spreading is that we should try to enjoy music the way a child does – full of **wonder** and with pure, **unprejudiced** amazement.

    1 If you are **in awe of** something, you *admire / cannot appreciate* it.

    2 You are likely to be full of **wonder** *on a beautiful mountain / in a dark room*.

    3 When you are **unprejudiced**, you have *an open / a closed* mind about something.

2 ▶ **4.13** Watch Daria van den Bercken play two pieces of music. How do you think she describes each piece? Circle your ideas.

    Piece 1 a melancholic   b relaxing
    Piece 2 a energetic   b romantic

3 ▶ **4.14** Watch Part 1 of the TED Talk. Answer the questions.

    1 Why was Daria van den Bercken surprised by the music she found on the Internet?

      a She didn't know Handel wrote keyboard music.   b It was extremely difficult to play.

    2 Why was she 'in awe' of the music?

      a because it was a mix of musical styles   b because it changed from sad to energetic

4 ▶ **4.15** Watch Part 2 of the TED Talk. Who does van den Bercken describe when she makes these claims? Tick (✓) the correct column.

	7- and 8-year-olds	11- and 12-year-olds
1 They're willing to listen to classical music.		
2 It's hard to get them to listen to classical music.		
3 The opinions of others matter to them.		
4 They listen to music with an open mind.		

CREATIVE THINKING

5 Daria van den Bercken wants everyone to enjoy music in the same way a child does. Think of something you are passionate about. How could you share your passion?

VOCABULARY IN CONTEXT

6 ▶ **4.16** Watch the clips from the TED Talk. Choose the correct meaning of the words.

7 Work in pairs. Discuss the questions.

1 Would you be comfortable talking to your work colleagues about your personal life?

2 For you, what counts more: being successful or being happy?

PRESENTATION SKILLS Providing background information

TIPS

During a presentation, it's often useful to include some information about your own background. This can help the audience understand why you're interested in the topic you're talking about.

8 ▶ **4.17** Watch the clip. What background information does van den Bercken provide?

a who first got her interested in learning the piano

b how she learned something new about a composer

c the first time she heard someone play Handel's music

9 ▶ **4.18** Now watch two other TED speakers. Match the speaker to the background information they give. One is extra.

1 A. J. Jacobs

2 Ann Morgan

a a meeting with a famous person

b an email that inspired them

c what they learned about themselves

10 Work in a group. Imagine you are going to give a presentation about your passion. What background information about yourself would you provide?

4.5 Musical choices

COMMUNICATE Desert island discs

1   Imagine you are going to spend a year alone on a desert island. You can choose four songs to take with you and listen to while you're there. Write your list below.

1 _____	3 _____
2 _____	4 _____

2   Look at the questions and prepare to answer them for each song on your list. Research any information you don't know.

> Who sings the song?
>
> Do you know who wrote it?
>
> When did you first hear it?
>
> Why is it special to you?
>
> What words would you use to describe the song?

3   Work in pairs. Use the questions above to interview each other. Ask for extra information.

4   Listen to each other's songs. Tell your partner your opinion.

DESCRIBING MUSIC

It makes me feel …   It sounds …   It reminds me of …   When I listen to it, I …

WRITING Describing a favourite song

5   Think of one more of your favourite songs. Explain how it makes you feel and why you like it. Does it remind you of anything or anyone special in your life?

> One of my favourite songs is 'Wake Up' by Arcade Fire. I like it because it's a really powerful and energetic song, and it makes me feel strong. It reminds me of my time at university.

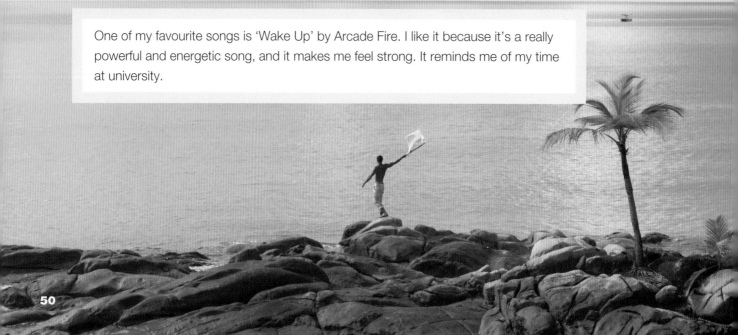

Good design

Colourful, contemporary
architecture at Rivers Academy,
London, welcomes visitors and
students

WARM UP

Look at the photo and read the caption. Discuss
the questions.

1 Do you like the design of the building in the
photo? Why? / Why not?

2 Does it make a difference to study or work in a
well-designed building?

3 What buildings do you enjoy being in because of
their design?

In this unit you:

- talk about design
- learn to use prepositions
  and adverbs of place
- watch a TED Talk by
  ROMAN MARS about
  good flag design

A piece of art on display at the Smithsonian's National Museum of the American Indian, Washington

5.1 Does it go?

VOCABULARY Design elements

1 These words can be used to describe visual design, including art. ~~Cross out~~ the word that does not belong in each category.

1 **colours**	bright	short	pale	vibrant	_____
2 **lines**	straight	happy	curved	thick	_____
3 **shape**	pale	round	triangular	square	_____
4 **size**	orange	tiny	large	huge	_____
5 **texture**	silky	empty	rough	smooth	_____
6 **contrast**	subtle	sharp	tall	dramatic	_____

2 Work in pairs. Add one more word to each category.

Pronunciation Sound and spelling

3 ▶ 5.1 Listen. Notice how the pronunciation of these pairs of letters change in different words, and depending on the surrounding letters. Listen again and repeat.

1 r<u>ou</u>gh   r<u>ou</u>nd

2 <u>or</u>ange   sh<u>or</u>t

3 l<u>a</u>rge   squ<u>a</u>re

4 t<u>a</u>ll   p<u>a</u>le

5 or<u>a</u>nge   vibr<u>a</u>nt

4 Which of the words in Exercise 1 could you use to describe the art in the picture? Do you like it? Why? / Why not? Discuss with a partner.

I like it. The colours are really vibrant.   Me too. I like the bright colours and the curved lines.

LISTENING A designer's advice

> **Listening for changes in topic**
> These are some of the phrases that we use to introduce a new topic in English.
>
> With/In regard to ....   Regarding ...
>
> As far as ... is concerned

5 ▶ **5.2** Sarah Lafferty is an interior designer. Listen and complete the quotation she uses.

'Have nothing in your houses that you do not know to be _____ or believe to be _____.'
William Morris

Sarah Lafferty

6 ▶ **5.2** Listen again. Circle the correct options to complete the sentences.

1 Sarah Lafferty's parents were *architects / interior designers*.

2 Lafferty studied *interior / textile* design at university.

3 She wants the houses she designs to reflect her *clients' / own* taste.

7 Look again at the quotation by William Morris in Exercise 5. What would you need to change in your own home to make this true? Discuss with a partner.

SPEAKING Talking about design

8 ▶ **5.3** Listen to the conversation. Do you think the people will buy the sofa?

A: What do you think of this one?

B: This one? Don't you think the colours are a bit too **bright**? **strong / vibrant**

A: No, I love the colours. And the shape is **perfect** for our living room. **ideal / just right**

B: Yeah, but I don't think it will **go with** the rest of our furniture. **match / look good with**

A: Why not?

B: Well, we don't have anything else that has yellow and pink stripes.

A: Our walls are yellow.

B: Yeah, but it's a very **pale** yellow. Can we look at something **light / soft**
else, please?

9 Practise the conversation with a partner. Practise again using the words on the right.

10 Work in pairs. Turn to page 161. What do you like and dislike about each piece of furniture?

I like the shape and the colours.

I agree. But I think they're too bright.

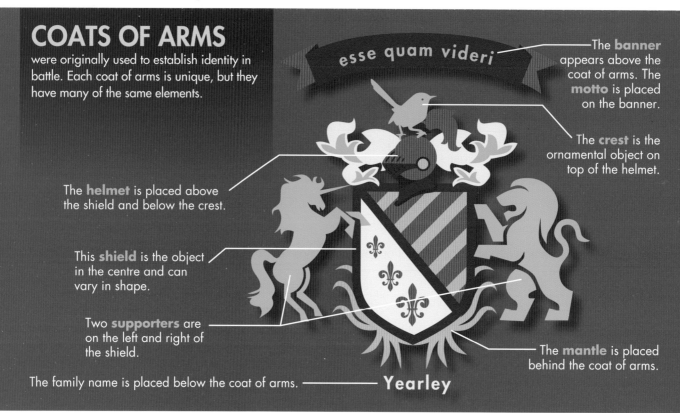

COATS OF ARMS were originally used to establish identity in battle. Each coat of arms is unique, but they have many of the same elements.

esse quam videri

The **banner** appears above the coat of arms. The **motto** is placed on the banner.

The **crest** is the ornamental object on top of the helmet.

The **helmet** is placed above the shield and below the crest.

This **shield** is the object in the centre and can vary in shape.

Two **supporters** are on the left and right of the shield.

The family name is placed below the coat of arms. — Yearley

The **mantle** is placed behind the coat of arms.

GRAMMAR Prepositions and adverbs of place

1 ▶ 5.4 Look at the infographic. What were coats of arms originally for?

2 ▶ 5.5 Listen to an expert explain the parts of a coat of arms. Circle the correct words.

  1 *All / Not all* coats of arms have a motto.

  2 Sometimes the motto is *below / on* the shield.

  3 The supporters are *always / usually* animals.

  4 The design on the shield *has / has no* meaning.

3 ▶ 5.6 Read the sentences in the Grammar box. Answer the questions (a–c).

4 Look at the infographic. Complete the sentences with these words and phrases. Add *of* where you need to.

above	around	at the bottom
in front	in the shape	on the left
on top	in the middle	

1 The unicorn is _____ the shield.

2 The family name is _____.

3 The crest is _____ a bird.

4 The bird is _____ the helmet.

5 The shield is _____ the coat of arms.

6 There is a border _____ the shield.

7 The shield is _____ the mantle.

8 The banner is _____ the shield.

PREPOSITIONS AND ADVERBS OF PLACE

1 There's a unicorn **on the left of** the shield.
2 There are three ornamental flowers **on the** shield.
3 There's a banner **at the top**.
4 The mantle is **behind** the coat of arms.

a Which sentences show prepositions of place?
b Which sentence shows an adverb of place?
c What do you need to add after the adverb to make it a preposition?

Check your answers on page 143 and do Exercises 1–2.

5 Complete the sentences with words and phrases from the Grammar box and Exercise 4. Add *of* where you need to.

1 When they took the painting off the wall, they found a secret door _____ it.

2 It's a simple design with a yellow sun _____ the picture and green grass _____ it.

3 Don't stand _____ me. I can't see the paintings, just the back of your head!

4 It's a sign to remind people to drive _____ the road while they are in Britain.

Pronunciation Word linking

6 ▶ 5.7 Listen. Notice how the consonant at the end of one word links to the vowel at the start of the next. Listen again and repeat.

1 This is a coat of arms.

2 Look at the design on the shield.

3 It's in the shape of an animal.

4 This motto's in Latin.

7 ▶ 5.8 Complete the information. Circle the correct words. Listen and check your answers.

> Most countries in Europe use similar road signs. This makes it easy for visitors to understand them. For example, a give way sign is ¹*in / on* the shape of an inverted triangle. It's white or yellow and has a red border ²*across / around* it. A traffic light sign is similar, but the wide part of the triangle is at the ³*middle / bottom*. There are three circles ⁴*inside / outside* the triangle. The one ⁵*at / in* the top is red. The one ⁶*in / of* the middle is yellow and the bottom one is green, just like a traffic light. There are no words ⁷*on / at* the sign.
>
>

8 Correct the mistake in each description.

1 A 'No parking' sign in the United States is a black *P* on a white circle. There is a red border behind the circle and a red line through the *P*.

2 A stop sign in Brazil is on the shape of an octagon. It is red and has the word *pare* (Portuguese for *stop*) written on it.

3 A 'Kangaroo crossing' sign in Australia is a yellow, diamond-shaped sign with a black image of a kangaroo below it.

SPEAKING Describing a coat of arms

9 You are going to design your own personal coat of arms. Look back at the coat of arms in the infographic. Decide on a motto and the different design elements. Draw your design, but don't show it to anyone.

10 Work in a group. Describe your coat of arms. Your group members will try to draw it.

> There are two supporters. The one on the left is a dolphin. The one on the right is a whale.

> OK. What shape is the shield?

11 Show your coat of arms to your group. Whose drawing is the closest to your original?

5.3 Symbol of a city

READING Chicago's much-loved flag

1 Look at the photo and read the third paragraph of the article. What do the three parts of Chicago's flag represent?

1 the white areas: _____   **2** the stripes: _____   **3** the stars: _____

Understanding main ideas

2 ▶ **5.9** Read the article. Circle the main idea.

a The flag of Chicago is important to the identity of the city and its people.

b The flag of Chicago is a best-selling souvenir for tourists.

c The flag of Chicago became famous after being featured on a radio show.

Understanding supporting quotes

3 Match each person to the statement that supports their quote.

1 Whet Moser
2 Ted Kaye
3 Roman Mars

a The Chicago flag is a symbol of pride for people in the city.
b People like Chicago more because it has a great flag.
c You can see the Chicago flag all around the city.

Understanding details

4 Circle **T** for true, **F** for false or **NG** for not given.

1 Chicago is one of few cities in the United States that has a flag.	**T**	**F**	**NG**
2 Whet Moser has a Chicago flag tattoo.	**T**	**F**	**NG**
3 The Chicago flag can be seen during some people's funerals.	**T**	**F**	**NG**
4 Experts in flag design like the Chicago flag.	**T**	**F**	**NG**
5 Roman Mars has lived in Chicago all his life.	**T**	**F**	**NG**

Understanding vocabulary

5 Circle the correct options to complete the sentences.

1 An example of a barber's **tool** is _____.
  a a customer   b a pair of scissors

2 If you have something **permanently**, you have it _____.
  a for a long time   b for a short time

3 A flag with a **bold** design is _____ to see or notice.
  a easy   b difficult

4 A design that is **distinctive** is _____ others.
  a similar to   b different from

5 **Symbolism** refers to what something _____.
  a looks like   b means or represents

6 What events in your town or city's history could be represented on a flag? Discuss with a partner.

The Chicago flag can be seen all around the city

CHICAGO'S MUCH-LOVED FLAG

1 Many cities in the United States have flags, but few are as loved as Chicago's. It can be seen all over the city – from its street corners to its skyscrapers. 'Today', says Whet Moser from
5 *Chicago* magazine, 'I went to get a haircut. When I sat down in the barber's chair, there was a Chicago flag on the box that the barber kept all his **tools** in. In the mirror, there was a Chicago flag on the wall behind me. When I left, a guy passed me who had
10 a Chicago flag on his backpack.' There is even a website called ChicagoFlagTattoos.com. It features interviews with, and photos of, people who love the flag so much that they want it **permanently** drawn on their bodies.

15 **2** The flag is also a **distinctive** symbol of Chicago pride. As flag expert Ted Kaye says, 'When a police officer or a firefighter dies in Chicago, often it's not the flag of the United States on his [1]coffin. It can be the flag of the city of Chicago. That's how deeply the flag has gotten into the [2]civic imagery of Chicago.' 20

3 Like any good flag, the Chicago flag's design is simple and its **symbolism** is clear. The white areas represent three Chicago neighbourhoods. The stripes represent the river and the lake. The stars represent important events in Chicago's history. 25 Its simple but **bold** design is [3]rated highly by flag experts and is probably also the reason it has become so popular.

4 Roman Mars moved to Chicago in 2005, and he too fell in love with the flag. Mars is the [4]host and 30 creator of *99% Invisible* – a popular radio show about design and architecture. He's sure that the love for the flag is not just because people love Chicago. In Mars's own words, 'I also think that people love Chicago more because the flag is so cool.' 35

---

[1] **coffin (n)** a box in which a dead person is buried
[2] **civic (adj)** related to a particular community

[3] **rate highly (phrase)** to have a very good opinion of
[4] **host (n)** someone who introduces a TV or radio programme

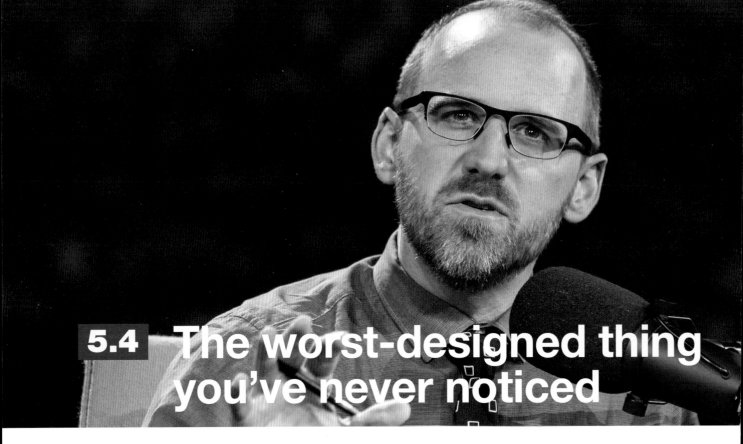

5.4 The worst-designed thing you've never noticed

TEDTALKS

1 Read the paragraph. Complete the definitions (1–4). You will hear these words in the TED Talk.

> **ROMAN MARS** tells stories about design on the radio. His **mission** is to get people to **engage with** designs they find **compelling** so that they begin to **pay attention to** all forms of design. His idea worth spreading is that a well-designed city flag can be an object of beauty, strengthen civic pride and have economic benefits.

1 A **mission** is something that someone feels they *need / don't need* to do.

2 If something is **compelling**, it is *interesting and exciting / ugly and boring*.

3 If you **engage with** something, you *ignore / show interest in* it.

4 When you **pay attention to** something, you *buy / concentrate on* it.

2 Look at the flags of Canada and San Francisco. What do you like about each design?

3 ▶ 5.10 Watch Part 1 of the TED Talk. Which flag does Roman Mars prefer? Why? Discuss with a partner.

4 Read the excerpt from Part 1 of the TED Talk. How is San Francisco different to Chicago? Think about what you read in *Chicago's much-loved flag* on page 57.

> 'So when I moved back to San Francisco in 2008, I researched its flag, because I had never seen it in the previous eight years I lived there.'

5 ▶ **5.11** Try to complete the notes below with these words. Watch Part 2 of the TED Talk to check your guesses.

bigger	colours	name	enlarge
middle	simple	simplify	writing

Five principles of flag design:	**To improve San Francisco's flag:**
1 Keep it _____ .	Remove the motto.
2 Use meaningful symbolism.	Remove _____ .
3 Use only two to three basic _____ .	_____ border.
4 Do not use _____ of any kind.	Make the phoenix (bird) _____ and move to _____ .
5 Be distinctive.	_____ or stylize the phoenix.

6 ▶ **5.12** Watch Part 3 of the TED Talk. Tick (✓) the statements that Roman Mars would probably agree with.

a City flags can bring people together.

b Pocatello has a terrible flag.

c A good flag should have a trademark symbol.

CRITICAL THINKING

7 To design a great flag, Roman Mars says you should first draw a rectangle this size to check that you can see the flag from a distance. Draw a flag you know in the rectangle. Based on this rule, does the flag have a good design?

VOCABULARY IN CONTEXT

8 ▶ **5.13** Watch the clips from the TED Talk. Choose the correct meaning of the words.

9 Work in pairs. Discuss the questions.

1 Do you ever complain in restaurants? What do you complain about?

2 Is there anything you're obsessed with? (e.g. an activity, a product, a kind of music)

PRESENTATION SKILLS Numbering key points

TIPS

Numbering the points in your talk (*one, two, three* or *first, second, third*, etc.) can help your audience follow your ideas more easily.

10 ▶ **5.14** Watch the clip. Notice how the points are numbered.

11 ▶ **5.15** Now watch clips of TED speaker A. J. Jacobs giving four reasons why a world family tree is important. Circle the numbers you hear.

1 One / First   **2** Two / Second   **3** Three / Third   **4** Four / Fourth

12 Work in a group. Think of three things you learned in this unit. Then share them using numbers.

5.5 Keeping it simple

COMMUNICATE Designing a new city flag

1 Work in a group. Look at these city flags. Which one do you like the most? Which one do you like the least? Why?

2 Work in pairs. You are going to design a new flag for your city. First, write down four or five things that your city is famous for. Think about famous places and historical events.

3 Work together to design and sketch your flag. Try to follow Roman Mars's design principles.

   1 Keep it simple.

   2 Use meaningful symbolism.

   3 Use only two or three basic colours.

   4 Do not use writing of any kind.

   5 Be distinctive.

4 Draw your flag on a bigger sheet of paper. Then present your flag to the class. Explain what the different parts of your flag represent and any other design choices you made.

TALKING ABOUT MEANING

What is the meaning of …?   It means …
What does … represent?   It represents …
What does … symbolise?   It symbolises …

WRITING Describing your country's flag

5 Think about your country's flag. Do some research and then write about the design and what the flag means.

> The design of my country's flag is very simple. It uses three colours – green, black and white. There are three vertical stripes and in the top left corner there is a …

6 Inspiring people

Educator and National Geographic Explorer Kakenya Ntaiya reads with students at her school in Kenya

WARM UP

Look at the photo and read the caption. Discuss the questions.

1 How would you describe the learning experience in this photo?

2 What makes a teacher inspiring?

3 Have you had any inspiring teachers?

In this unit you:

- talk about inspirational people
- learn to report what people say
- watch a TED Talk by **JARRETT J. KROSOCZKA** about the events that inspired his career

A father watches as his son launches a model rocket

6.1 They changed my life

VOCABULARY Sources of inspiration

1 ▶ 6.1 Complete the sentences with these words. Listen and check your answers.

changed	gave	inspired
showed	supported	was

1 'When I met my best friend Maria, she completely _____ my life.'

2 'My biology teacher, Mrs Chang, _____ me to become a scientist.'

3 'My first boss _____ a great role model for me when I first started work.'

4 'My mother _____ me that it's possible to stay positive even in difficult times.'

5 'I was lucky that my parents always _____ my career in music.'

6 'My grandfather always _____ me great advice when I was young.'

2 Change two or three of the sentences in Exercise 1 to make them true for you.

3 Work in pairs. Read your sentences to each other. Ask questions as you listen.

My older brother was a great role model for me when I was a child.

Yeah? In what way?

LISTENING My inspiration

> **Listening for expressions of uncertainty**
> It is common for English speakers to use certain words or phrases to indicate uncertainty. Common words include:
>
> | probably | possibly | maybe | perhaps |

4 ▶ **6.2** Franklin Chang Díaz is a former NASA astronaut. Who does he describe as his number one hero? Listen and circle the correct answer.

a his science teacher **b** a famous astronaut **c** his father

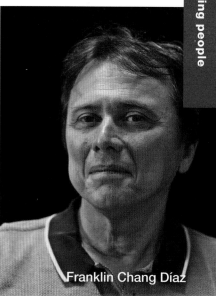
Franklin Chang Díaz

5 ▶ **6.2** Listen again. Circle **T** for true or **F** for false.

1 As an astronaut, Chang Díaz went into space only once. **T F**

2 Chang Díaz became interested in space when he was a child. **T F**

3 Chang Díaz's father was a scientist. **T F**

4 Chang Díaz is certain he is an inspiration for others. **T F**

Pronunciation *that*

6 ▶ **6.3** Listen and notice the pronunciation of *that* in these sentences. In which sentence is it pronounced differently? Why?

1 He was a guy **that** was not afraid of anything.

2 I feel **that** this was not part of my plan.

3 And **that** is part of the way it should be.

SPEAKING Talking about an inspirational person

7 ▶ **6.4** Listen to the conversation. What was the music teacher's advice?

A: When did you graduate from university?

B: **About three** years ago. I kind of miss being a student. **A couple of / Just a few**

A: I know what you mean. What **did you study**? **subject did you do / was your degree in**

B: Business administration. What about you?

A: I studied music.

B: Yeah? Why did you choose that?

A: I had a great music teacher at school.
She **really inspired me**. **was really inspiring / was an inspiration**

B: That's cool.

A: Yeah. She always **told me to** follow my passion in life. **advised me to / said that I should**
It was really great advice.

8 Practise the conversation with a partner. Practise again using the words on the right.

9 Think of three inspiring people. Tell your partner why they inspire you.

> My cousin is really inspiring. She's a doctor and she works all over the world, often in really difficult conditions. She's amazing!

6.2 Inspiring words

THE WORLD'S MOST INSPIRATIONAL PEOPLE

A recent survey identified 50 of the world's most inspiring people. Here are the top three.

NELSON MANDELA

1918–2013
Former President of South Africa

" Education is the most powerful weapon which you can use to change the world. "

MAHATMA GANDHI

1869–1948
Leader of independence movement in India

" You must be the change you wish to see in the world. "

STEVE JOBS

1955–2011
Cofounder, chairman and CEO of Apple, Inc.

" Innovation distinguishes between a leader and a follower.

THESE PEOPLE ALSO MADE THE LIST: Leonardo da Vinci (Italy), Anne Frank (Germany), Frida Kahlo (Mexico), Bob Marley (Jamaica), Coco Chanel (France), Stephen Hawking (England), Martin Luther King Jr. (US)

GRAMMAR Reported speech

1 ▶ 6.5 Look at the infographic. What else do you know about these people?

2 ▶ 6.6 Listen to a man talking about two people he admires. Complete the table.

Who does he admire?	Why does he admire them?
1	
2	

3 Read the sentences in the Grammar box. Answer the questions (a–c).

REPORTED SPEECH

Frida Kahlo said, 'I **paint** myself because I **am** so often alone.'

Frida Kahlo said (that) she **painted** herself because she **was** so often alone.

a What happens to the verb tenses when the sentence is reported?

b What word do we sometimes add before the reported words?

c What change is there to the pronoun in the reported sentence?

Check your answers on page 145 and do Exercises 1–2.

4 Look at how some quotations by Oscar Wilde are reported. What do you think were his original words?

1 Oscar Wilde said that he could resist everything except temptation.

Oscar Wilde said, 'I …

2 He said that experience was simply the name we gave our mistakes.

3 He said that whenever people agreed with him he always felt he must be wrong.

4 He said that life imitated art far more than art imitated life.

5 Report these famous quotations.

1 'I have a dream.' Martin Luther King

2 'I want to be alone!' Greta Garbo

3 'That's one small step for man, one giant leap for mankind.' Neil Armstrong

4 'Learning never makes the mind tired.' Leonardo da Vinci

Pronunciation Giving emphasis

6 ▶ 6.7 Which word(s) should we emphasize in the quotations in Exercise 5? Underline the word(s). Listen and check. Practise saying the sentences.

LANGUAGE FOCUS Reporting what people say

7 ▶ **6.8** Study the examples in the Language focus box

REPORTING WHAT PEOPLE SAY

'I admire Frida Kahlo.'	He **said** He **told me**	**(that)** he **admired** Frida Kahlo.
'I don't know much about her.'	He **said** He **told me**	**(that)** he **didn't know** much about her.
'Follow your dreams.' 'Don't be afraid.'	He **told me to follow** my dreams. He **told me not to be** afraid.	

For more information and practice, go to page 146.

8 Circle the correct options to complete the sentences.

1 My teacher *said / told* me not to interrupt while other people are talking.

2 My father *said / told* that he had two jobs when he was a student.

3 Her older brother *said / told* her to take her piano lessons more seriously.

4 My coach *said / told* me that I was his most promising new player.

5 Our professor always *said / told* us that there is no success without failure.

9 Rewrite the sentences.

1 'Think carefully about your future.'
My dad told me _____

_____ .

2 'I want to lead our country some day.'
My sister said _____

_____ .

3 'Don't make the same mistake twice.'
The teacher told her _____

_____ .

4 'I don't want to stand in your way.'
My mother told me _____

_____ .

5 'I don't worry about the little things.'
My grandfather said _____

_____ .

10 ▶ **6.9** Find and correct four mistakes in the text. Listen and check your answers.

At eighteen years of age, Frida Kahlo was involved in an accident that changed her life. Her school bus hit a streetcar and she broke her back. She had to spend many months in bed. She told a friend that she wants to die because she was in so much pain and so bored. However, during this time, she discovered her love of painting. Kahlo painted many self-portraits. She once told that she painted herself because she was the subject she knew best. After her recovery, she met painter Diego Rivera and later married him. He recognized her talent and said her to keep painting. Her colourful work is sometimes described as folk art. However, Kahlo told that her work described the reality of her life.

Frida Kahlo

SPEAKING Getting advice

11 Think of two people who gave you advice. Share the advice with a group. Can others guess who gave you the advice (and if you took it)?

Someone told me to take up acting in high school.

Was it a teacher?

6.3 Inspiring lives

READING Drawing your own success

1 Work in pairs. Look at the book on the right. What do you think it's about?

2 ▶ 6.10 Read the article quickly to check your idea. Do you think you would enjoy reading the book?

Understanding main ideas

3 Read the article again. Choose the best heading for each paragraph.

   1 Paragraph 3   a Early love of art   b A fantasy world

   2 Paragraph 4   a Celebrating success   b A writer is born

   3 Paragraph 5   a Success at last   b Funny fan mail

Understanding sequence

4 Number the events in the order they happened (1–5).

   a Krosoczka published his first book. _____

   b Krosoczka began to volunteer with sick children. _____

   c Krosoczka graduated from art school. _____

   d Krosoczka's first-grade teacher attended his book signing. _____

   e Jarrett J. Krosoczka got a fortune cookie that said he would be successful. _____

Understanding details

5 Match the two parts to make sentences.

   1 The Teenage Mutant Ninja Turtles   **a** adopted him.

   2 Krosoczka's grandparents   **b** taught him to read.

   3 Krosoczka's parents   **c** send him fan mail.

   4 Eric   **d** inspired him to write children's books.

   5 Mrs Alisch   **e** were never around.

   6 Kids around the country   **f** were his best friends.

Understanding vocabulary

6 Circle the correct options to complete the sentences.

   1 If you **encourage** someone you want them to _____ .

     a keep trying   b stop what they are doing

   2 If you **gave up** during a competition, you _____ .

     a quit   b won

   3 Students are likely to **celebrate** when they _____ an exam.

     a pass   b fail

   4 You might send **fan mail** to _____ .

     a a family member   b a famous person you like

7 What do you think are the best things about being a children's author? Discuss with a partner.

Jarrett J. Krosoczka offers to sign a book for a young fan

DRAWING YOUR OWN SUCCESS

1 On Jarrett Krosoczka's fourteenth birthday, his grandparents gave him a gift – a drawing table. During dinner that night, the ¹fortune in his fortune cookie said, 'You will be successful in your work.'
5 He taped it to the table.

2 Krosoczka came from a troubled family – his parents were never around and he had few friends. His best friends at the time were the Teenage Mutant Ninja Turtles and other
10 characters he read about in books. When he was in the third grade, his grandparents adopted him. 'They loved me so much', he says, 'and they supported my creative efforts.'

3 Even as a young boy, Krosoczka loved
15 drawing and writing stories. He was lucky in that people **encouraged** him both at home and at school. One teacher in particular stood out for him, his first-grade teacher, Mrs Alisch. 'I can just remember the love that she offered us as
20 her students', he recalls. Krosoczka is now a successful artist. His readers love his books and he receives **fan mail** from kids all over the world. Interestingly, he still draws on the same table that

he got on his fourteenth birthday, and the fortune is still taped to it. 25

4 When he was seventeen, he ²volunteered at a camp for sick children called Hole in the Wall and met Eric, a child with leukemia. Eric sadly didn't live to see his sixth birthday. It was an inspirational experience that Krosoczka said changed his life – 30 it was the ³pivotal moment that made him want to write picture books for children.

5 After graduating from art school, Krosoczka struggled to publish his work, but he never **gave up**. He eventually published his first book, *Good* 35 *Night, Monkey Boy* – a story about a young, energetic boy who never wants to go to bed. His local newspaper **celebrated** the news and he signed copies of the book at a local book shop. Many of the people who inspired him were present 40 at the event, including his friends, grandparents and even several of his teachers. Mrs Alisch pushed to the front of the ⁴queue and proudly said, 'I taught him how to read.' It was a very special moment for Krosoczka. 45

---

¹ **fortune (n)** a piece of paper (sometimes inside a Chinese cookie) that has a quote or prediction about your future

² **volunteer (v)** to work for no money

³ **pivotal (adj)** very important

⁴ **queue (n)** a line of people waiting for something

6.4 How a boy became an artist

TED TALKS

1 Read the paragraph. Complete the definitions (1–3). You will hear these words in the TED Talk.

> **JARRETT J. KROSOCZKA** is an author and **illustrator**. In his TED Talk he describes a **compliment** he received that made a **colossal** difference to his life. His idea worth spreading is that inspiration often comes to us in unexpected ways and that we can use our own talents to inspire others.

   1 The **illustrator** of a book is the person who *writes it / draws the pictures*.

   2 If you give a **compliment**, you say something *nice / bad* about someone.

   3 A **colossal** failure is a *very big / really small* failure.

2 ▶ **6.11** Watch Part 1 of the TED Talk. Circle the correct answers.

   1 Who was Jack Gantos?

     a an author

     b a teacher

   2 How did Gantos inspire Jarrett J. Krosoczka?

     a He complimented Krosoczka on his drawing.

     b He helped Krosoczka write a story.

   3 What did Krosoczka start to do after school?

     a write letters to famous authors

     b write his own stories

3 ▶ 6.12 Watch Part 2 of the TED Talk. Tick (✓) each box to show if the statement refers to Mr Greenwood or Mr Lynch. Some statements refer to both.

	Mr Greenwood	Mr Lynch
a complimented him on his drawing	☐	☐
b said he should be the school cartoonist	☐	☐
c asked him to stop drawing in class	☐	☐
d told him to forget everything he learned	☐	☐

4 ▶ 6.13 Watch Part 3 of the TED Talk. Work in pairs. Explain why each thing below is important to Krosoczka.

a an email that said, 'Nice work!'   **b** the date June 12, 2001   **c** a Monkey Boy birthday cake

CRITICAL THINKING

5 Work in pairs. Think of examples of the following and tell your partner. What makes a good compliment?

- a compliment you received that was important to you
- a compliment you gave someone else

VOCABULARY IN CONTEXT

6 ▶ 6.14 Watch the clips from the TED Talk. Choose the correct meaning of the words.

7 Work in pairs. Complete the sentences in your own words.

1 I once got in trouble when I was … because …

2 I'm very proud of … because …

PRESENTATION SKILLS Using your voice effectively

TIPS

You can make your presentation clearer and more memorable by using your voice effectively. You can raise or lower your voice, stress words, vary your speed, pause, or even change your voice to indicate you're quoting another person.

8 ▶ 6.15 Watch the clip. Notice how Krosoczka speaks very softly when he's telling the story of the visiting author. Why do you think he does this?

9 ▶ 6.16 Now watch two other TED speakers. What does each person do with his voice?

1 A. J. Jacobs

a He speeds up and stresses key words.   b He slows down and speaks very softly.

2 Roman Mars

a He makes his voice much higher.   b He slows down and pauses between words.

10 Work in pairs. Read the text below in these different ways. Which do you think is the most effective?

> emphasizing key words   pausing at key moments   using your grandmother's voice

My grandmother was an inspiration to me. One day I was upset with a grade I got at school and she said, 'Just do your best. No one should expect more than that.' I looked at her for a moment but didn't say a word. And deep in my heart, I knew she was right.

6.5 A world of inspiration

COMMUNICATE A dinner party

1 Work alone. Write a list of people that you find inspirational. Think about people from the following categories.

political figures	athletes	musicians	entertainers
writers	artists	explorers	scientists

2 Work in pairs. Imagine you are having a small dinner party for eight people (including you and your partner). You can invite anybody you like from your lists of inspirational people. Decide on six people to invite. Give reasons for your answers.

FINDING OUT WHAT SOMEONE KNOWS

Do you know …?   Have you heard of …?   Are you familiar with …?

3 Now decide on the seating plan. You want an interesting party with lively conversation. Decide who should and shouldn't sit where and why.

4 Work with another pair. Describe your dinner party and give reasons for your seating plan.

WRITING Describing an inspiring person

5 Who do you think is inspirational? Write about them. It could be a famous person or someone you know personally. What makes the person so inspirational?

My older sister Rebecca is a great role model for me. She is very ambitious and she worked very hard to become a successful scientist. She showed me that anything is possible if you try your best.

MODEL PRESENTATION

1 Complete the transcript of the presentation using these words.

around	bright	gave	little	much
on	relaxed	said	showed	told

Today, I want to tell you about a person who made a huge difference in my life – my first teacher, Mrs Daniels. When I was young, I was extremely shy and had very [1]_____ self-confidence. I remember being so nervous on my first day at school. But Mrs Daniels was so kind and friendly, I soon forgot about all that. In that first class, Mrs Daniels asked us all to draw a picture of ourselves to put [2]_____ the classroom wall. She walked [3]_____ the classroom patiently helping everyone. When she got to my desk, she looked at my picture and [4]_____ 'Wow! Look at those [5]_____ colours! That's great!' I immediately felt [6]_____. But that wasn't all. Mrs Daniels was my teacher for one year, and she helped me become a lot more confident. She always praised us and encouraged us to express ourselves. She [7]_____us not to worry about giving the wrong answers in class and [8]_____ us how to learn from our mistakes. Even today, I still remember all the advice that Mrs Daniels [9]_____ me. I think without her, I would be a different person. I owe her so [10]_____.

Thank you for listening.

2 ▶ **P.2** Watch the presentation and check your answers.

3 ▶ **P.2** Review the list of presentation skills from units 1–6 below. Which does the speaker use? Tick (✓) each skill used as you watch again.

Presentation skills: units 1–6		
The speaker …		
• uses questions to signpost ☐		• provides background information ☐
• personalizes the presentation ☐		• numbers key points ☐
• closes the presentation effectively ☐		• uses their voice effectively ☐

YOUR TURN

4 You are going to plan and give a short presentation to a partner about a great teacher you once had. Use some or all of the questions below to make notes.

> - What was the teacher's name?
> - What did they teach?
> - Why were they a great teacher?
> - What advice did the teacher give you?
> - How did the teacher affect your life?

5 Look at the Useful phrases box. Think about which ones you will need in your presentation.

USEFUL PHRASES

Giving background information	Describing inspiration
When I was ... / As a child ... / Before I ...	changed my life / enouraged me / gave me advice / showed me / supported me / was a role model

Reporting what someone said	Describing effects
said that / told me that / advised me to	I'll always remember ... / Since then, I ... I'll never forget ...

6 Work in pairs. Take turns giving your presentation using your notes. Use some of the presentation skills from units 1–6. As you listen, tick (✓) each skill your partner uses.

Presentation skills: units 1–6

The speaker ...
- uses questions to signpost ☐
- personalizes the presentation ☐
- closes the presentation effectively ☐
- provides background information ☐
- numbers key points ☐
- uses their voice effectively ☐

7 Give your partner some feedback on their talk. Include two things you liked, and one thing he or she can improve.

> That was great. You used your voice really well and provided lots of background information. Next time, try to smile a bit more.

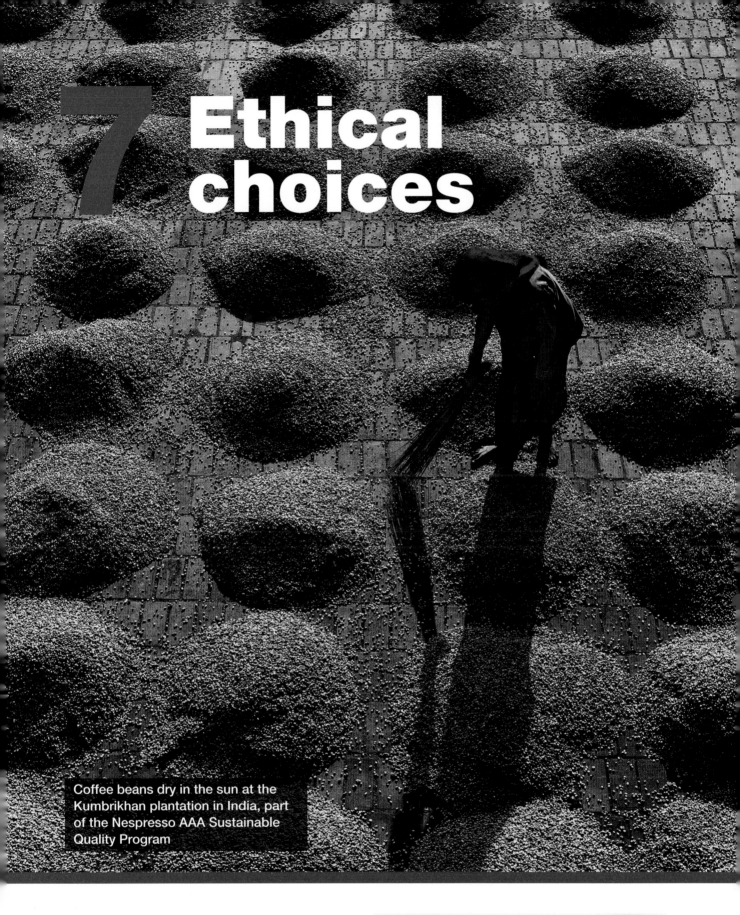

7 Ethical choices

Coffee beans dry in the sun at the Kumbrikhan plantation in India, part of the Nespresso AAA Sustainable Quality Program

WARM UP

Look at the photo and read the caption. Discuss the questions.

1 What makes coffee 'ethical'?

2 Do you think it's important to produce food ethically?

3 Do you make any ethical choices when you shop?

In this unit you:

- talk about ethical choices
- make predictions about the future
- watch a TED Talk by **ANDRAS FORGACS** about a way to produce meat and leather more ethically

An organic farm in British Columbia, Canada

7.1 It's better for the environment

VOCABULARY Ethical food choices

1 ▶ **7.1** Complete each definition with these words. Listen and check your answers.

fair-trade	free-range	organic
locally-produced	genetically modified	sustainable

1 _____ food is grown naturally, without using any special chemicals.

2 On _____ farms, animals are not kept in cages and can move around.

3 _____ food is grown using technology to change the food's size, colour, taste, etc.

4 _____ food production aims to provide better trading and working conditions for farmers in developing countries.

5 By choosing _____ food, you reduce the distance the food needs to travel. This helps the environment.

6 _____ food production aims to preserve the world's natural resources for the future.

Pronunciation Intonation in questions with options

2a ▶ **7.2** Listen to this question. Notice the intonation on the options.

Are you a vegetarian or a meat eater?

2b ▶ **7.3** Listen. Mark the intonation in these questions. Then take turns asking and answering the questions.

1 Do you usually buy organic or non-organic fruit?

2 Is it easy or difficult to find fair-trade foods where you live?

3 Is genetically modified food a good idea or a bad idea?

4 Do you think it's important or not important to buy free-range eggs?

LISTENING Sustainable chef

Identifying main ideas in fast speech
Many native speakers talk quickly but will often slow down to emphasize key points. Focusing on these slower parts of speech can help identify the speaker's main message.

3 ▶ **7.4** Barton Seaver is a chef and environmentalist. What did he once work as in Africa? Listen and circle the correct answer.

a a farmer   **b** a fisherman   **c** a trader

4 ▶ **7.4** Listen again. Complete the sentences with the words you hear.

1 '_____ is how the vast majority of us interact with our resources.'

2 'Environmentalism is so often thought of as this _____ idea.'

3 'But _____ is full contact environmentalism.'

5 Work in pairs. Can you explain in your own words what Seaver means by each quote in Exercise 4?

Barton Seaver

SPEAKING Talking about ethical choices

6 ▶ **7.5** Listen to the conversation. Why did the woman change to organic food?

A: I think that's all I need. How about you?

B: Let me just get some apples, then I'll be **ready**. done / finished

A: Why don't you get these? They look nice.

B: Oh, I only eat organic fruit and vegetables now.

A: Really? **Why**? Why's that / How come

B: I decided I didn't want to eat food that is grown using chemicals. I heard it's not very good for you.

A: **That makes sense**. Fair enough / I can understand that

B: And it's better for the environment.

A: But does that mean you have to **pay higher prices**? pay more / spend more

B: Not necessarily. It depends where you shop.

7 Practise the conversation with a partner. Practise again using the words on the right.

8 Work in pairs. Which of these things do you buy more often? Why?

• farmed or wild fish
• locally-produced or imported food
• cheaper or better quality fruit and vegetables

7.2 What does the future hold?

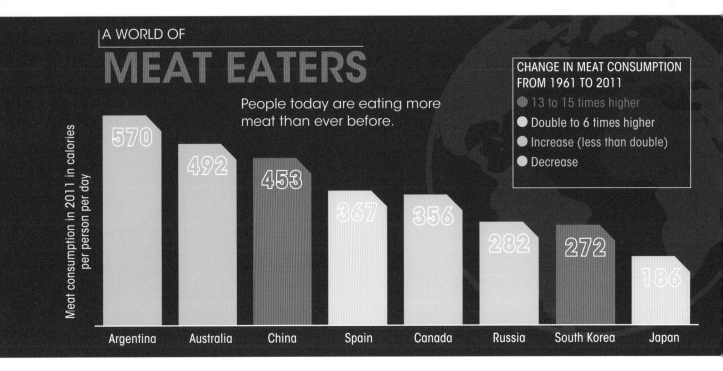

A WORLD OF

MEAT EATERS

People today are eating more meat than ever before.

Meat consumption in 2011 in calories per person per day

| Argentina | Australia | China | Spain | Canada | Russia | South Korea | Japan |
| 570 | 492 | 453 | 367 | 356 | 282 | 272 | 186 |

CHANGE IN MEAT CONSUMPTION FROM 1961 TO 2011
- 13 to 15 times higher
- Double to 6 times higher
- Increase (less than double)
- Decrease

GRAMMAR *will* for predictions

1 ▶ 7.6 Look at the infographic. Which two countries saw the biggest increase in meat consumption? What do you think was the reason? Discuss with a partner.

2 ▶ 7.7 An expert is talking about the data. Listen and circle the correct options.

  1 Population increase by 2050: *15% / 35%*

  2 Future global demand for meat: *increasing / decreasing*

  3 Increase in demand for meat: *100% / 150%*

3 Complete sentences 1 and 2 with the information from Exercise 2. Then answer the questions (a–c).

WILL FOR PREDICTIONS

1 We think the population **will** increase by _____ per cent.

2 The demand for meat **will** _____ by _____ per cent.

3 We **won't** be able to meet the increased demand.

a Do the sentences refer to future plans or things you imagine happening in the future?

b What form of the verb do we use after *will*?

c What is the contracted form of *will not*?

Check your answers on page 146 and do Exercises 1–2.

4 ▶ 7.7 Choose the correct options to complete the sentences. Listen again to check your answers.

  1 Today, people around the world *are eating / will eat* more meat than ever before.

  2 Do you think this trend *is continuing / will continue* in the future?

  3 Every day, there *are / will be* 228,000 more people on the planet.

  4 By 2050, many more people *are able to / will be able to* buy meat regularly.

  5 In the next 30 years, there *is / will be* a huge rise in the number of people demanding meat.

  6 In the future, it *won't be / isn't* easy to meet the increased demand for meat.

5 Which sentences in Exercise 4 are predictions for the future?

LANGUAGE FOCUS Discussing the future

6 ▶ **7.8** Study the examples in the Language focus box.

DISCUSSING THE FUTURE

In the future, more people **will be** vegetarian.
There **won't be** enough water to produce food the way we do now.

The price of food **will definitely / probably be** higher in the future.
There **definitely / probably won't be** enough water to produce all the food we need.

Will it **have** an effect on the environment?	Yes, it **will**. / No, it **won't**.
When will the world's population **reach** ten billion people?	It **will reach** ten billion **by** around 2050 / **in** about 30 years.

For more information and practice, go to page 147.

7 Put the words in the correct order to make predictions.

1 double / need to / says / will / The UN / our food production / we

2 eat meat / definitely / People / won't / so frequently / be able to

3 will / We / probably / in cooking / more insects / start to use

4 definitely / Restaurants / vegetarian options / offer / more and better / will

5 won't / Being a vegan / an / probably / be / life choice / unusual

6 New technology / in the desert / allow us / might / to / grow food

8 ▶ **7.9** Find and correct three mistakes in the text. Listen and check your answers.

According to a recent report, climate change has started to affect farmers around the world. Although some crops will definitely grow better in a warmer world, others won't probably do so well.

The report predicts that the production of crops like corn, wheat and rice will start to decrease by 2030. They probably decline by up to two per cent for each decade after that.

Other crops, such as fruit and nut trees, will also be affected. Almonds need long periods of cool weather. Without it, trees won't flower. Other crops that will be definitely under threat in the next few decades are grapes, cherries and apples.

Pronunciation *will*

9a ▶ **7.10** Listen to six sentences. Notice the different ways we pronounce *will*.

9b ▶ **7.10** Look at the audioscript on page 164. Why do you think *will* is pronounced more strongly in sentences 5 and 6? Listen again and repeat.

SPEAKING Predicting future habits

10 Write five questions to ask a partner about their predictions for food in the next twenty years. Think about how eating habits will change, the cost and availability of food, etc.

11 Work in pairs. Take turns asking and answering the questions. Give reasons for your answers.

Do you think people in your country will eat more meat in the future?

No, I don't. People in this country already eat a lot of meat.

7.3 A kinder way

READING Leather from a lab

1 How many leather products do you own? Discuss with a partner.

2 Read the first paragraph of the article. What is the problem with leather?

Understanding details

3 ▶ 7.11 Read the article. Circle **T** for true, **F** for false or **NG** for not given.

1 Many animals are killed to make leather.	T	F	NG
2 Demand for leather is increasing.	T	F	NG
3 Biofabrication is already used in medicine.	T	F	NG
4 Animals feel pain when scientists take their cells.	T	F	NG
5 Biofabrication could be used to grow meat.	T	F	NG

Understanding process

4 Look at the diagram. Number the sentences 1–8.

a Scientists grow the cells in a lab. _____

b Scientists can tan the hide. _____

c Thicker sheets are formed. _____

d Scientists spread the cells and form thin sheets. _____

e Scientists take cells from an animal. _____

f The thin sheets are layered. _____

g The leather can be dyed and finished. _____

h The leather is made into different products. _____

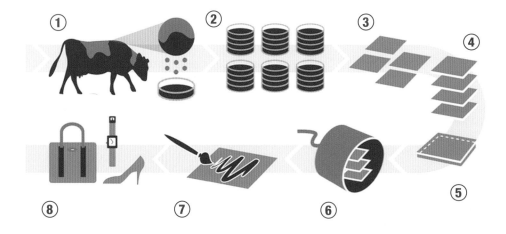

Understanding vocabulary

5 Match the **bold** words from the article with their definitions.

1 range   **a** a room where scientific experiments take place

2 cell   **b** able to do something well without wasting time or energy

3 lab   **c** an extremely small part of an animal or plant

4 layer   **d** a number of different things

5 efficient   **e** to arrange one on top of another

6 Would you wear biofabricated leather? Would you eat biofabricated meat? Discuss with a partner.

Over a billion animals a year are killed
to make leather products like these

LEATHER FROM A LAB

Leather is a hugely popular material for a **range** of products: shoes, jackets, bags, wallets – the list goes on. But this popularity comes at a price. The global leather industry kills over a billion animals
5 every year. This has caused many to ask the question: is it possible to meet the global demand for leather but not do any harm to animals? A process called biofabrication may be the answer.

Biofabrication is not new; it is already commonly
10 used in medicine. Biofabrication techniques are used to grow body parts like ears, skin and bones for [1]transplants. But it can also be used to make other products, such as leather. Biofabricated leather has many advantages. Scientists will be
15 able to make it with whatever qualities they want, such as extra softness, greater strength, or even different colours and patterns.

But how exactly does biofabrication work? To grow leather, scientists begin by taking some

cells from an animal, not hurting the animal in any 20 way. They then isolate the cells and grow them in a **lab**. This process takes millions of cells and expands them into billions. Next, the scientists take the cells and spread them out to form thin sheets. These thin sheets are then **layered** 25 to combine into thicker sheets. After that, the scientists can [2]tan the hide. Anyone can then [3]dye and finish the leather and design it in any way they like – into bags, wallets or shoes.

Andras Forgacs supports biofabrication. He says 30 it may even be a 'natural [4]evolution of manufacturing for mankind'. We will be able to make the products we need in a more **efficient**, responsible and creative way. And biofabrication is not just about leather – it's possible the technique could also be 35 used to grow meat. While this may sound crazy, Forgacs certainly doesn't think so. 'What's crazy', he says, 'is what we do today.'

---

[1] **transplant (n)** an operation in which a body part is replaced
[2] **tan the hide (phrase)** to turn animal skin into leather
[3] **dye (v)** to change the colour of something using special liquid
[4] **evolution (n)** a process of gradual, natural change over time

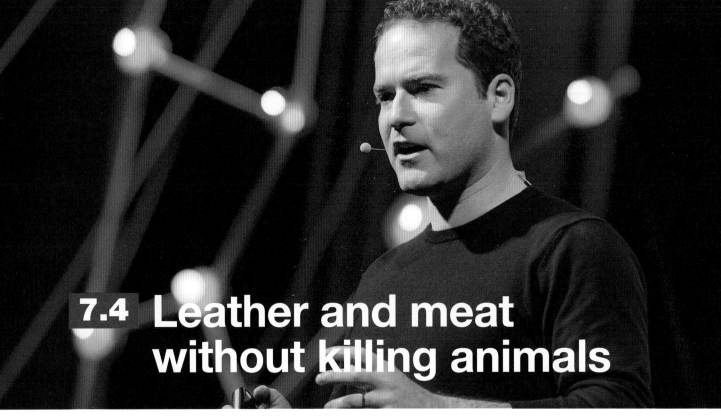

7.4 Leather and meat without killing animals

TEDTALKS

1 Read the paragraph. Complete the definitions (1–4). You will hear these words in the TED Talk.

When **ANDRAS FORGACS** started a company to 3D-print human **tissues** and **organs**, people thought he was crazy. But after some success, he realized he could also grow products like meat and leather to avoid the **slaughter** of animals. Forgacs' idea worth spreading is that we can be more efficient and **humane** by getting meat and leather from tissues grown in a lab.

1 **Tissues** are materials that *living things / machines* are made from.

2 An example of a human **organ** is your *brain / foot*.

3 When you **slaughter** an animal, you *save / kill* it.

4 A **humane** person is *kind and gentle / mean and angry*.

2 Look at this slide from Andras Forgacs' TED Talk. What do you think the infographic describes?

7
BILLION
PEOPLE

60 BILLION
LAND ANIMALS
2012

10
BILLION
PEOPLE

100 BILLION
LAND ANIMALS
2050

3 ▶ 7.12 Watch Part 1 of the TED Talk. Tick (✓) the reasons why Andras Forgacs is concerned about having so many farm animals on the planet.

a The animals will use large amounts of land and water.

b The animals will produce even more greenhouse gases.

c It will cause many wild animals to become extinct.

d Diseases will spread more easily.

4 ▶ 7.13 Watch Part 2 of the TED Talk. Why does Forgacs think producing leather is a good place for biofabrication to begin? Tick (✓) each reason he mentions.

a It's widely used.

b It's beautiful.

c It's cheap.

d It's part of our history.

e It's simple to grow.

f It's strong.

5 ▶ **7.14** Watch Part 3 of the TED Talk. Match the two parts of the notes to make sentences.

Benefits of biofabricated leather

1 It is just like normal leather because it is made from
2 It doesn't have
3 It can be grown in the shape of
4 It is not limited to the shape of
5 We can control

a a cow or alligator.
b its properties.
c the same cells.
d a wallet or handbag.
e hair, scars or insect bites.

CRITICAL THINKING

6 Which of these groups do you think would support biofabrication? Why? / Why not? Discuss with a partner.

vegetarians   farmers   fashion designers

VOCABULARY IN CONTEXT

7 ▶ **7.15** Watch the clips from the TED Talk. Choose the correct meaning of the words.

8 Work in pairs. Discuss the questions.

1 What are you convinced will happen in the future? What are you not sure about?
2 Does your place of work or study have any good facilities (e.g. gym, café, library)?

PRESENTATION SKILLS Creating effective slides

> **TIPS**
>
> Take the time to make your presentation slides as effective as possible. The following tips can help you:
>
> Keep the background plain. Use strong, contrasting colours.
> Do not use too much text. Keep any graphics or images simple.

9 ▶ **7.16** Watch part of Andras Forgacs's TED Talk. Notice how effective Forgacs' slide is.

10 ▶ **7.17** Now watch Forgacs show another slide. Do you think it's effective? Why? / Why not? Use the tips in the Presentation skills box to help you decide.

7.5 Looking ahead

COMMUNICATE Arguing for and against

1 Work in a group. The local government is considering opening a biofabrication lab in your city. Brainstorm some arguments for and against opening the lab. Write some notes in the table below. Consider these factors:

| how it affects jobs | how the meat looks and tastes | public perception |
| the effect on animals | people's openness to change | what it could lead to |

Arguments for the biofabrication lab	Arguments against the biofabrication lab

2 Split into two groups. Group A is in favour of the biofabrication lab. Group B is against it. You are going to give a presentation to argue your position. Choose three or four of the strongest arguments. Prepare some slides to help get your points across.

3 Present your arguments and your slides to another group. Take notes as you listen.

ACKNOWLEDGING A POINT

That's a good point, but …   I see what you mean, but …
I can see your point, but …

WRITING Predicting the future of food

4 Are you optimistic or pessimistic about the future of food? Support your idea with at least three predictions of what you think the future will be like.

I am optimistic about the future of food. I think scientists will continue to find new, creative ways to feed our population. They will also find ways to make food more nutritious.

8 Better cities

The High Line, an old railway line in New York, is now a public park

WARM UP

Look at the photo and read the caption. Discuss the questions.

1 Have you been to or heard about the High Line? What do you think of it?

2 Can you think of any similar examples of positive change in other cities you know?

3 Do you have ideas for how you could improve your city like this?

In this unit you:

- talk about features of a city
- use phrasal verbs
- watch a TED Talk by **ALESSANDRA OROFINO** about how technology can help solve urban problems

Vancouver, Canada

8.1 What makes a great city?

VOCABULARY Features of a city

1 Complete the table using these words.

amusement parks	galleries	lively
ancient	historic centre	multicultural
concert halls	industrial estate	suburbs

Areas of a city	Things to enjoy	Words to describe a city
residential area riverfront	museums flea markets	bustling peaceful

2 Work in pairs. Add two more words to each column.

3 What are the best things about your town or city? Why? Discuss with a partner.

I really like the riverfront area. It's a great place to hang out.

I agree. I like the cafés and restaurants there.

LISTENING Living abroad

> **Listening for time expressions**
> Identifying time expressions can help you understand if a speaker is talking about the past, present or future.
>
> **Past**: in 2002, five years ago, last year, last August
> **Present**: these days, nowadays, now, right now, at the moment
> **Future**: next year, in two years, in 2025, one day

Claire Street

4 ▶ **8.1** Claire Street is talking about three different countries she has lived in. Listen and write the names of the countries.

1 She grew up in a town called Whitworth in _____ .

2 She moved to _____ when she was 21.

3 Now she lives in _____ .

5 ▶ **8.1** Listen again. How does Claire describe the three different places? Which place do you think is her favourite?

Pronunciation Showing enthusiasm

6a ▶ **8.2** Listen to the way the speaker shows enthusiasm.

1 Singapore was a great place to live.

2 Sydney is a wonderful place.

3 There's so much to do in Sydney.

6b Change the places in Exercise 6a for somewhere you know. Practise saying the sentences in pairs. Remember to show enthusiasm.

SPEAKING Talking about where you live

7 ▶ **8.3** Listen to the conversation. What do the two people like about living in Brisbane?

A: How do you like living in Brisbane so far?

B: Oh, I love it. It's such a **busy** place. You grew up here, didn't you? **multicultural / lively**

A: Actually, I was born in a small town near here called Toowoomba, but I moved here about seven years ago.

B: What's your favourite **part of the city**? **area / place**

A: Well, I really like the South Bank Parklands. I know a few nice **restaurants** there. **cafés / shops**

B: Yeah?

A: Yeah, it's a great place to **hang out** with friends. **meet up / spend time**

B: Cool. I should check it out sometime.

8 Practise the conversation with a partner. Practise again using the words on the right.

9 Work in pairs. What city would you like to live in one day? Why?

I'd love to live in Madrid one day. I'd like to learn Spanish.

But why Madrid and not another Spanish city?

8.2 Happy cities

THE BEST CITIES IN THE WORLD

These four cities rank among the top ten happiest in the world. What makes each city's residents so happy?

DUBAI, UNITED ARAB EMIRATES
- a high standard of living
- an excellent transport system
- world-class shopping

AUCKLAND, NEW ZEALAND
- excellent restaurants
- a bustling city centre
- a multicultural population

MONTERREY, MEXICO
- a high standard of living
- a bustling city centre
- an excellent transport system

AARHUS, DENMARK
- closeness to nature
- variety of restaurants
- sense of community

GRAMMAR Phrasal verbs

1 ▶ **8.4** Look at the infographic. Which of these cities would you like to live in?

2 ▶ **8.5** Listen to two people talking about Monterrey, Mexico. Why did the man like living there? Complete the sentences.

  1 The man grew up in *Aarhus / Monterrey* .

  2 He liked hanging out with his friends on the *beach / riverfront*.

  3 In the past, he got around by *bus / car*.

3 ▶ **8.6** Read the sentences in the Grammar box. Choose the correct options to complete a–e.

PHRASAL VERBS

Inseparable

I **grew up** in this neighbourhood. The bus is the best way to **get around**. What do you **look for** in a city?	The park is a good place to **hang out with** friends. I **meet up with** my friends every weekend. I'm **looking forward to** visiting Dubai.

Separable

They need to **clean up** their city. They need to **clean** their city **up**. Let's **check out** some new plays. Let's **check** some new plays **out**.	They need to **clean** it **up**. ~~They need to clean up it.~~ Let's **check** them **out**. ~~Let's check out them.~~

a Phrasal verbs *always have two / sometimes have three* parts.
b With *inseparable / separable* verbs we always use the verb and the particle together.
c With separable verbs you never put the *pronoun / noun* after the particle.
d 'Look at' and 'go out' are *separable / inseparable* verbs.
e 'Put on' and 'take off' are *separable / inseparable* verbs.

Check your answers on page 147 and do Exercises 1–2.

4 Complete the questions using a phrasal verb from the box.

> get around   grow up
> look for   hang out with

1 Where did you _____?

2 Is it easy to _____ by public transport in your city?

3 Where's a fun place to _____ your friends?

4 What do you _____ in a place to live?

Pronunciation Stress in phrasal verbs

5a ▶ 8.7 Listen to the questions from Exercise 4. Do we stress the verb or the particle in each sentence? Which sentence is different?

5b Work in pairs. Ask the questions from Exercise 4 and answer with your own information.

6 ▶ 8.8 Complete the information. Use a dictionary to help you. Listen and check your answers.

San Sebastián, Spain, must be one of the most beautiful cities in the world. It's a fantastic place to live, but it's also a great place for tourists to visit.

Chill [1]*off / out / down* on one of its four main beaches, eat [2]*off / out / by* at one of its many restaurants, or head [3]*up / to / against* the amusement park to get the best view of the city. Whatever you end [4]*up / in / off* doing, you'll have a memorable time.

There are always cultural events going [5]*on / in / at* in the city. Check [6]*down / out / up* a museum, take [7]*off / of / in* some live theatre, or spend some time at one of its many festivals. In fact, with Wroclaw in Poland, the city was named European Capital of Culture in 2016.

7 Complete the phone conversation using the correct form of the phrasal verbs in Exercise 6.

A: How's it going?

B: Great, thanks. We were quite tired when we arrived yesterday, so we [1]_____ at the hotel for a few hours before going out.

A: What's it like there?

B: It's very lively. There's always something [2]_____.

A: So what did you do on your first day?

B: In the afternoon, we [3]_____ the city centre to [4]_____ the shops.

A: Did you [5]_____ spending lots of money?

B: Not really. It's all quite cheap. In the evening, we [6]_____ at a local restaurant and [7]_____ some traditional music in a bar.

SPEAKING Talking about places to go

8 Work in pairs. Discuss the questions and note your answers.

Where's the best place in your city to …?

eat out on a budget _____

get around by bicycle _____

spend a rainy afternoon _____

chill out and do nothing _____

9 Join another pair and compare your ideas.

8.3 Connecting citizens

READING Having a say about your city

1 Do you think people who live in cities are happier than other people? Discuss with a partner.

2 ▶ **8.9** Read the article. What does Alessandra Orofino think?

Understanding purpose

3 What is the main purpose of the article? Circle the correct answer.

   a to explain the benefits of living in cities

   b to highlight problems of cities and offer a possible solution

   c to show what Rio de Janeiro learned from other cities

Understanding main ideas

4 Match each paragraph with its main idea.

1 Paragraph 1	**a**	People are becoming disconnected from their cities.
2 Paragraph 2	**b**	As cities grow, there are fewer close communities.
3 Paragraph 3	**c**	Cities around the world are growing.
4 Paragraph 4	**d**	Cities have their good points, but they also have problems.
5 Paragraph 5	**e**	Orofino hopes other cities will start a project like hers.
6 Paragraph 6	**f**	Alessandra Orofino started an organization to help involve Rio citizens in the running of their city.

Understanding details

5 Circle **T** for true, **F** for false or **NG** for not given.

1 Rio de Janeiro is the fastest-growing city in Brazil.	**T**	**F**	**NG**
2 The number of people living in cities around the world is rising.	**T**	**F**	**NG**
3 In cities around the world, election turnouts are increasing.	**T**	**F**	**NG**
4 People in Rio de Janeiro are required to vote by law.	**T**	**F**	**NG**
5 Alessandra Orofino started Meu Rio in 2011.	**T**	**F**	**NG**
6 Members of Meu Rio receive news updates via the Internet.	**T**	**F**	**NG**
7 Meu Rio has more than 200,000 members.	**T**	**F**	**NG**

Understanding vocabulary

6 Complete the paragraph with the **bold** words and phrases from the article.

When a country holds a(n) ^{1}_____ , it's an opportunity for ^{2}_____ to ^{3}_____ and to make their voices heard on relevant issues. In about two dozen countries, including Argentina, Greece and Australia, people are ^{4}_____ to participate in the process. If they choose not to, they have to ^{5}_____ or perform community service.

7 Does your town or city have similar problems to those described in the article? Discuss with a partner.

HAVING A SAY ABOUT YOUR CITY

1 Urban activist Alessandra Orofino's home city of Rio de Janeiro is one of the world's megacities. With a population of over eleven million, Rio has grown extremely quickly over the last 60 years.

5 But Rio is not unique. Cities around the world are growing at similar speeds. Today, around half the world's population lives in cities, and nearly two billion more people are expected in the next twenty years.

10 **2** Cities are growing because of all the benefits they offer, such as [1]convenience, culture and jobs. But [2]in spite of the advantages, Orofino believes that modern city life is far from ideal.

3 According to Orofino, people are becoming 15 increasingly disconnected from the cities they live in. **Election** [3]turnouts in cities around the world are falling. In Rio, for example, voting is **required** by law. However, in one election, nearly 30 per cent of people did not **vote**; they stayed at home 20 and chose to **pay a fine** instead.

4 Orofino also believes that cities cause us to be disconnected from one another. As new buildings are built, many public spaces disappear. Without these places, it's difficult for people to [4]socialize, make friends and form a close and happy community. 25

5 Orofino believes that getting **citizens** to work together and be more involved with the running of their cities is hugely important. To this end, Orofino [5]co-founded a group called Meu Rio. Meu Rio is an online network that makes it easier for 30 Rio citizens to [6]have their say about the running of the city. As part of the network, people receive news updates and are able to participate in important decisions about the future of their city.

6 Meu Rio has been a huge success. More than 35 200,000 Rio citizens are now part of this online community. Orofino is hopeful that projects like hers will become common in cities around the world and will start what she calls 'a participation revolution'.

---

[1] **convenience (n)** a situation where things are easy to do
[2] **in spite of (phrase)** although something else exists
[3] **turnout (n)** the number of people who vote in an election

[4] **socialize (v)** to meet and talk to different people
[5] **co-found (v)** to start an organization together with another person
[6] **have your say (phrase)** to give your opinion about something important to you

8.4 | It's our city. Let's fix it

TEDTALKS

1 Read the paragraph. Match each **bold** word with its meaning (1–4). You will hear these words in the TED Talk.

> **ALESSANDRA OROFINO** tells us that over 30 per cent of people in **developing** countries live in **slums**. However, in spite of their problems, she calls cities 'the greatest **invention** of our time'. She works with an organization that helps Rio de Janeiro's citizens start campaigns that will bring change to their city. Her idea worth spreading is that we can combine technology and 'people power' to **fix** big problems in the world's cities.

1 something that has been newly created: _____

2 a place with little money and few industries: _____

3 a poor and crowded area of a city: _____

4 to repair something: _____

2 ▶ 8.10 Watch Part 1 of the TED Talk. Match the information to complete the statistics.

1 The percentage of the world's population that lives in cities.   **a** 80%

2 The percentage of global energy consumption that occurs in cities.   **b** 75%

3 The percentage of global gas emissions that come from cities.   **c** 54%

4 The percentage of Meu Rio members who are aged 20–29.   **d** 40%

3 ▶ 8.11 Watch Part 2 of the TED Talk. Alessandra Orofino describes three members of her organization. Complete the notes.

Bia	Jovita	Leandro
• _____-year-old girl • government wanted to destroy her _____ to build a parking lot* • used Meu Rio to start a campaign • the government changed their minds	• her _____ went missing around _____ years ago • found out Rio had no system to find missing persons • used Meu Rio to start a campaign to create a system • secretary of security received _____ emails • a police unit was set up	• lives in a slum • created a _____ project • received an order from the government saying he had to _____ the area in two weeks • used Meu Rio to start a campaign • the government changed their mind

*parking lot = car park

4 ▶ **8.12** Watch Part 3 of the TED Talk. Choose the correct option to complete the sentences.

  1 Orofino says the stories make her happy because _____ .

  a she sees good things starting to happen   b she knew the people personally

  2 Next, Orofino wants to _____ .

  a share what she has learned   b develop the Meu Rio technology even further

CRITICAL THINKING

5 Could the 'people power' solutions that Orofino discusses work in your city? Why? / Why not?

VOCABULARY IN CONTEXT

6 ▶ **8.13** Watch the clips from the TED Talk. Choose the correct meaning of the words.

7 Work in pairs. Discuss the questions.

  1 Do you think your friends and family care about the environment?

  2 What is your opinion of 24/7 communication? Are there any negatives?

PRESENTATION SKILLS Using anecdotes

TIPS

A speaker may use an anecdote to make a point. Anecdotes can be powerful tools. An audience often reacts emotionally to a true story.

8 ▶ **8.14** Watch part of Alessandra Orofino's talk. Notice how effective her anecdote is.

9 ▶ **8.15** These TED speakers used anecdotes to make a point. Do you remember what they were? Match each speaker with the correct anecdote. Watch the clips to check your answers.

  1 Ann Morgan   **a** a time when someone famous visited their school

  2 Daria van den Bercken   **b** a time when they discovered something on the Internet

  3 Jarrett J. Krosoczka   **c** a time when they learned something about themselves

10 Work in a group. Choose one of these topics. Prepare and tell a short anecdote.

  inspiration   kindness   friendship   honesty   change

  I once ordered a coffee, but when I went to pay I realized I didn't have my purse. The woman behind me in the queue offered to buy the coffee for me. It was so kind!

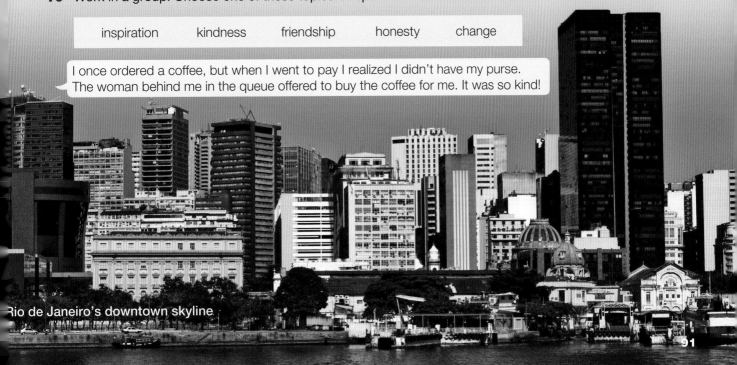

Rio de Janeiro's downtown skyline

8.5 Creative solutions

COMMUNICATE Let's fix this!

1 Your city has a problem with lost pets. When a pet gets lost, there is no way to track or find it. You're going to design a smartphone app to help. Work in a group. Brainstorm ways an app could help solve the problem.

> An app could help you track your pet's location.

> Good idea. How would it work?

2 Choose the best ideas and work together to design your app. Complete the notes below.

> Name of app:
>
> What can it do?
>
> How does it work?

GIVING EXAMPLES

for example, …	for instance, …	such as …

3 Work with another group. Compare your ideas. Which app do you think would be best at solving the problem?

WRITING Describing a change for the better

4 Imagine you can make one change – big or small – to your city. What would you do? Why?

> One problem with my city is that it doesn't use enough renewable energy. Most of the city's power comes from an old gas power station, and I don't think this is good for the environment. I'd like to …

A dog is fitted with an electronic tracking device

9 Giving

A professional hairdresser gives a
homeless man a free haircut, New York

WARM UP

Look at the photo and read the caption.
Discuss the questions.

1 What do you think of the example of
'giving' you can see in the photo?

2 What other examples can you think of
where people give their time for free?

3 What ways do you (or could you) use
your skills to help people?

In this unit you:

- talk about fundraising and
good causes
- discuss making offers and
describing possible future
events
- watch a TED Talk by **JOY
SUN** about a different way
to help people

A young pink river dolphin is rescued from illegal traders, Amazon River, Peru

9.1 It's for a good cause

VOCABULARY Fundraising

1 Look at the phrases. Cross-out the option that doesn't belong.

1 donate	money	time	social work
2 raise	volunteers	money	awareness
3 make	a cause	a donation	a difference
4 hold	a fundraiser	a charity	an event
5 support	a cause	a charity	money
6 sponsor	somebody	an event	money

2 Work in pairs. Think of at least one charity for each category in the table.

Health	Environment	Animal welfare

3 Choose one or two charities from Exercise 2. Explain what they do.

Save the Children raises awareness to give children around the world a good start in life.

Yes, they raise money for better health care and education.

LISTENING My fundraising adventure

> **Understanding directions**
> The nouns *north*, *south*, *east* and *west* are also often used as adverbs to describe a direction of movement.
>
> go north   head south   sail east   fly west

4 ▶ **9.1** Listen to Neil Glover talking about a time he raised money for charity. What did he do to raise money?

   a He drove across the north of India.

   b He drove from north to south India.

   c He drove around the south of India.

5 ▶ **9.1** Listen again. Circle **T** for true or **F** for false.

   1 There were about thirteen teams.   **T**   **F**

   2 The journey took eight days.   **T**   **F**

   3 Glover's friends and family donated money online.   **T**   **F**

   4 Glover's team raised $170,000.   **T**   **F**

Neil Glover with local children during his fundraising journey

Pronunciation Linking with /w/ and /j/

6a ▶ **9.2** Listen to the extract. Notice how we sometimes link two words with a /w/ or a /j/ sound.

   We ͜ used social media to ͜ ask our friends…
   (/j/ over "We used"; /w/ over "to ask")

6b ▶ **9.3** Work in pairs. Which words will link with a /w/ or /j/ sound? Listen and check. Practise saying the sentences.

   1 The event raised a lot of money.   **3** They all encouraged us.

   2 They wanted to ask us questions.   **4** We met a man who asked us to play cricket.

SPEAKING Talking about good causes

7 ▶ **9.4** Listen to the conversation. What are the two people talking about?

   A: Oh, my sister just texted me. She asked me to sponsor her for a charity run.

   B: What type of charity?

   A: She's trying to raise money **to help save the rainforest**.   for an animal charity / for cancer research

   B: That's great!

   A: Yeah. Last year, she ran a marathon to help raise awareness. She also **set up a website**.   held a fundraising event / gave a talk

   B: So, how much do you think you'll **give**?   donate / contribute

   A: Hmm. I think I'll donate £20.

   B: OK. Well, if you give £20, I will too. **After all**, it's for a really good cause.   I mean / It seems to me

8 Practise the conversation with a partner. Practise again using the words on the right.

9 Think about a time you helped a charity or did something to help someone. Explain how you helped.

   Last year, I volunteered at a hospital. I read books to young children.

9.2 I'll help!

GIVING ONLINE

Statistics show that fundraising online can generate more donations than traditional methods. Costs are also lower – both in terms of time and money spent.

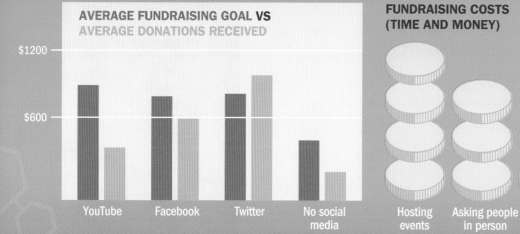

AVERAGE FUNDRAISING GOAL VS
AVERAGE DONATIONS RECEIVED

$1200
$600

YouTube   Facebook   Twitter   No social media

FUNDRAISING COSTS
(TIME AND MONEY)

Hosting events   Asking people in person   Phone calls   Sending letters   Social media

---

GRAMMAR *will* for offers and first conditionals

1 ▶ 9.5 Look at the infographic. What are two benefits of online fundraising? What is the most effective way of raising money online?

2 ▶ 9.6 Two people are talking about fundraising. Listen and complete the sentences.

   1 The man is raising money for a local _____ charity.

   2 The man is using _____ to collect donations.

   3 His friend says he will donate _____ dollars.

3 Read the sentences in the Grammar box. Choose the correct options to complete a–d.

4 Cross out the incorrect *will* (or *'ll*) in each sentence.

   1 If I will win the lottery, I'll give half of it to charity.

   2 I'll support you for your sponsored run if you will remind me.

   3 If you'll come on Saturday, I'll help you with your French.

   4 I'll visit Granny in hospital if I'll have time.

   5 If they will decide to support our charity, it will make a big difference.

Pronunciation Intonation with conditional sentences

5 ▶ 9.7 Listen and check your answers to Exercise 4. Notice how the intonation rises and then falls when the sentence starts with an *if* clause. Practise saying the sentences.

WILL FOR OFFERS AND FIRST CONDITIONALS

I'**ll do** it later today.

If you **donate** $50, I'**ll reach** my target of $1,000.

a Sentence *1 / 2* is an offer with *will*.

b Sentence *1 / 2* is a first conditional sentence.

c The first conditional uses *the present simple / will* in the *if* clause and *present simple / will* in the main clause.

d We use the first conditional for a *possible future / factual present* situation.

Check your answers on page 149 and do Exercises 1–2.

LANGUAGE FOCUS Making offers and describing possible future events

6 ▶ **9.8** Study the examples in the Language focus box.

MAKING OFFERS AND DESCRIBING POSSIBLE FUTURE EVENTS

I need help planning the event.	OK. I'**ll help** you.
I'**ll help** you **if** I **have** enough time. I'**ll give** you a hand **if** you **need** another person.	**If** I **have** enough time, I'**ll help** you. **If** you **need** another person, I'**ll give** you a hand.
We **won't have** enough people **if** you **don't help**.	**If** you **don't help,** we **won't have** enough people.
If I **give** £20, **will** you **give** the same amount?	Yes, I **will**. / No, I **won't**.

For more information and practice, go to page 149.

7 Match each sentence with the offer (a–e).

1 Jill isn't here yet.

2 We need $100 to reach our fundraising goal.

3 We need two more volunteers this weekend.

4 Can someone give me a lift to the event?

5 I don't understand what this charity does.

a OK, I'll donate $20 more.

b Sure, I'll take you.

c I'll explain it to you.

d I'll call her.

e OK, we'll come on Saturday.

8 ▶ **9.9** Complete the information. Circle the correct options. Listen and check your answers.

With the One Today app giving is easy. You get details of a different charity sent to your smartphone every day. If you ¹*decide / will decide* to donate, the app ²*send / will send* money directly to that day's charity.

You can customize the app, too. If you ³*add / will add* details about your preferences, the app ⁴*send / will send* information about different charities based on your interests. Many donations are just a dollar. The app's developers feel that more people will give money if the donations ⁵*are / will be* small.

9 Complete the sentences with your own ideas. Compare with a partner.

1 A: I'm thinking of volunteering at the hospital at weekends.
   B: Great! If you do, I'll
   _____ .

2 A: Do you think we should hold our fundraiser at 3.00 pm or 7.00 pm?
   B: Definitely at 7.00. If you hold it at 3.00,
   _____ .

3 A: What's the advantage of using social media to raise money for charity?
   B: If you use social media,
   _____ .

SPEAKING Planning an event

10 Work in a group. You are going to hold an outdoor fundraising event for a charity. Decide on a charity and then plan the event. Discuss these questions.

- How will you advertise the event?
- When and where will it be held?
- What activities will there be?
- What will each person's responsibilities be?

11 Create a backup plan in case these things happen. What will you do in each case?

It rains.   Nobody comes.
Nobody wants to donate.

If it rains, we'll have it on a different day.

Yeah, we'll try to move it to the following weekend.

9.3 Donation revolution

READING Giving on the go

1 Read the lesson title. What do you think the article is mainly about? Discuss with a partner.

2 ▶ 9.10 Read the article. Check your prediction.

Understanding purpose

3 Circle the option that describes the main purpose of each paragraph.

Paragraph 1
  a gives an example of a relief effort that benefited from new technology
  b explains how bad the Haiti earthquake was for the people there

Paragraph 2
  a describes how to donate using a charity's website
  b compares fundraising methods in the past with those in the present

Paragraph 3
  a explains the effect social media has had on fundraising
  b describes how to raise money using Facebook

Paragraph 4
  a compares the advantages and disadvantages of two new apps
  b gives examples of new ways of donating

Understanding details

4 Circle **T** for true, **F** for false or **NG** if the information is not given in the article.

1	The 2010 Haiti earthquake was the biggest in the country's history.	**T**	**F**	**NG**
2	In 2010, the American Red Cross raised $22 million in less than one week.	**T**	**F**	**NG**
3	After the Haiti earthquake, people donated money using their mobile phones.	**T**	**F**	**NG**
4	Charities raise more money through social media than through their own websites.	**T**	**F**	**NG**
5	Charity Miles raises money for charity while you're running.	**T**	**F**	**NG**
6	SnapDonate donates money every time you take a selfie.	**T**	**F**	**NG**

Understanding vocabulary

5 Complete the sentences using the **bold** words from the article.

1 The way charities raise money has changed due to _____ in technology.

2 Charity Miles is an example of a(n) _____ new app.

3 The 2010 Haiti earthquake is an example of a natural _____ .

4 The use of new technology has had a huge _____ on the speed of fundraising.

5 Earthquakes can cause a lot of _____ .

6 Read paragraph 4 again. Which app do you think would be more effective at raising money? Discuss with a partner.

UN soldiers help evacuate Haitian children from a refugee camp after the 2010 earthquake

GIVING ON THE GO

1 In 2010, a huge earthquake hit Haiti, causing the deaths of over a hundred thousand people and millions of dollars' worth of **damage**. The international community [1]jumped into action to
5 provide aid. On this occasion, funds were raised with amazing speed – within a week of the quake, the American Red Cross had raised $22 million. The reason? People were donating via their mobile phones.

10 **2** Technological **advances** have changed how charities work. Gone are the days when someone knocked on your front door and politely asked you to make a donation. In today's world of computers, smartphones and tablets, charities can now reach
15 more people than ever before.

3 Social media in particular has had a great **impact** on charity fundraising. News of **disasters** spreads quickly around the world. This enables charities to raise money extremely quickly, as in
20 Haiti. And the quicker aid can be delivered, the more lives can be saved. Individual fundraising has also benefited. Most people are now so well-connected through sites like Facebook that asking people to contribute to your chosen cause is easier than ever.

4 New, **innovative** ways of donating are being 25 thought up all the time. For example, if you want to support a good cause and keep fit at the same time, you can use an app called Charity Miles. The app can track the distance you run or cycle. For every kilometre you cover, the app's sponsors 30 will make a donation to a charity of your choice. There's also SnapDonate, which allows users to donate simply by taking a photo of a charity's [2]logo with their smartphone. The app recognizes the logo and allows users to immediately make 35 a donation through their phones. This cuts out the need for entering payment details on charity websites, and makes the process of donating small amounts to multiple charities much simpler.

5 Apps like these are growing in number, and 40 that can only be a good thing. In the future, it's likely that we'll all be able to give to our favourite causes more easily and more often.

---

[1] **jump into action (v)** to act quickly   [2] **logo (n)** a symbol or design used to represent a company

9.4 Should you donate differently?

TEDTALKS

1 Read the paragraph. Match each **bold** word with its meaning (1–4). You will hear these words in the TED Talk.

> **JOY SUN** is a **veteran** aid worker who has **dedicated** her career to helping the poor in developing countries. Her idea worth spreading is that there may be more value in giving money directly to poor people, for needs the **recipients** identify themselves, rather than **investing** in aid programmes.

1 people who receive something: _____

2 given time and effort to: _____

3 very experienced: _____

4 putting money into something: _____

2 ▶ **9.11** Watch Part 1 of the TED Talk. Tick (✓) each statement that Joy Sun now believes.

a It can be a good idea to give cash directly to poor people.

b Aid workers do more good for poor people than they can do for themselves.

c Poor people are poor partly because they don't make good choices.

3 ▶ **9.12** The table shows what happened in three countries when poor people received cash. Watch Part 2 of the TED Talk. Circle the correct words to complete the notes.

Uruguay	Sri Lanka	Kenya
• Pregnant women bought better *food / clothing*. • Women gave birth to healthier babies.	• Men invested in their *businesses / homes*.	• People invested in a range of assets˙. • Farming and business income *increased / decreased*.

˙**assets (n)** things that are useful and valuable to own

4 ▶ **9.13** Look at the graph. Does it show a successful or unsuccessful aid programme? Discuss with a partner. Watch Part 3 of the TED Talk to check your answer.

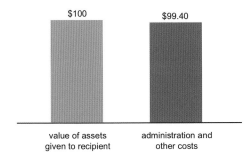

$100

$99.40

value of assets given to recipient

administration and other costs

5 ▶ **9.14** Watch Part 4 of the TED Talk. Circle the correct words to complete the summary.

GiveDirectly sends [1]*food / money* directly to the poor. So far the organization has helped [2]*1,000 / 35,000* people in Kenya and Uganda. Cash is sent to families in [3]*one-time / monthly* payments. The organization looks for the [4]*poorest / youngest* people in the poorest places. Joy Sun wants other aid organizations to think more about how they give and whether it might be more useful to give cash directly.

CRITICAL THINKING

6 Has Joy Sun's talk changed the way you think about giving to charity? Why? / Why not?

VOCABULARY IN CONTEXT

7 ▶ **9.15** Watch the clips from the TED Talk. Choose the correct meaning of the words.

8 Work in pairs. Discuss the questions.

    1 Are there any training programmes you would like to do?

    2 Would you use websites (e.g. social media) if you had to pay a fee?

PRESENTATION SKILLS Using supporting evidence

TIPS

In any presentation, it's important to support any points you make with evidence. For example, you could choose to:

quote an expert   quote some research   tell an anecdote

9 ▶ **9.16** Watch the clip from Joy Sun's TED Talk. Notice how she uses research to support her argument.

10 ▶ **9.17** Watch the clips. Match each speaker with the type of supporting evidence they use.

    1 Munir Virani   **a** tells an anecdote.

    2 A. J. Jacobs   **b** quotes some research.

    3 Andras Forgacs   **c** gives a statistic.

11 Work in a group. Each person must choose one of these topics to talk about for 30 seconds. As part of your talk, use some supporting evidence.

a good charity to support   a good place to volunteer
something good your company does   why giving time is better than giving money

A boy in Aceh, Indonesia, carries aid dropped by helicopter after the 2004 Indian Ocean Tsunami

9.5 Make a difference

COMMUNICATE Choosing a charity

1 Six charities are asking for donations. Turn to page 157 and read the information.

2 Work in a group. You have £100 to donate to one or more charities. Decide as a group who to give to, and how much to give.

> I think we should give some to Tsunami Relief.

> Maybe we should give to a local charity. It will help our community.

3 Work with another group. Present your ideas. Give reasons for your decision.

EXPLAINING REASONS		
Let me tell you why.	Let me explain why.	Let me give you the reason.

WRITING Describing a charity

4 Think about a cause or a charity that you support or think is a good cause. Consider these questions.

What does the charity do?

What are donations used for?

Why do you think it's a good cause?

5 Use the questions in Exercise 4 to write about the charity.

> I support the charity Sustrans. It's a charity that works to make it easier for people to travel by foot, bike or public transport. I think it's a great cause that can really make a difference. If people can use their cars less, it will be good for the environment.

MODEL PRESENTATION

1 Complete the transcript of the presentation using the words in the box.

ate out	check out	definitely	grew up	in
largest	locally	museums	suburbs	to

Today, I'm going to tell you about a great city that I visited last year – Toronto. Toronto is the most populous city in Canada. According [1]_____ the 2011 census, Toronto had a population of around three million people, and it's the fourth [2]_____ city in North America. It's a really lovely and cosmopolitan place. I stayed for a week with my friend Josh, who [3]_____ in Toronto. He lives in the [4]_____, but I visited the downtown area almost every day. There are so many things to do and places to see. I visited a lot of [5]_____ and art galleries and in the evenings I [6]_____ at some great restaurants. Toronto is also well known for its music scene – I managed to [7]_____ some really cool bands while I was there. My favourite place though was St Lawrence Market. According to *National Geographic*, it is the world's best food market and I could see why. You can spend hours there looking at and trying some of the [8]_____-produced food. [9]_____ the future, I'm hoping to visit again. When I finish university, I'd love to be able to find a job there and make Toronto my home. It [10]_____ won't be easy, but who knows?

Thank you so much.

2 ▶ P.3 Watch the presentation and check your answers.

3 ▶ P.3 Review the list of presentation skills from units 1–9. Which does the speaker use? Tick (✓) each skill used as you watch again.

Presentation skills: units 1–9		
The speaker …		
• uses questions to signpost ☐	• uses their voice effectively ☐
• personalizes the presentation ☐	• tells an anecdote ☐
• closes the presentation effectively ☐	• uses supporting evidence ☐
• provides background information ☐	• uses an effective slide ☐
• numbers key points ☐	

YOUR TURN

4 You are going to plan and give a short presentation to a partner about a city you've visited, or a city you'd like to visit. Use some or all of the questions below to make some notes.

> • What's the name of the city?
> • Where is it exactly?
> • What's special about it?
> • What did you do there? / What would you like to do there?

5 Look at the Useful phrases box. Think about which ones you will need in your presentation.

USEFUL PHRASES

Places in a city	Adjectives to describe a city
galleries, markets, museums, riverfront, suburbs, theatres	bustling, lively, modern, multicultural

Phrasal verbs	Future hopes
eat out, check out, hang out, get around	I'd love to ... / Hopefully, I'll ...

6 Work in pairs. Take turns giving your presentation using your notes. Use some of the presentation skills from units 1–9. As you listen, tick (✓) each skill your partner uses.

Presentation skills: units 1–9

The speaker ...
- uses questions to signpost ☐
- personalizes the presentation ☐
- closes the presentation effectively ☐
- provides background information ☐
- numbers key points ☐
- uses their voice effectively ☐
- tells an anecdote ☐
- uses supporting evidence ☐
- uses an effective slide ☐

7 Give your partner some feedback on their talk. Include two things you liked, and one thing he or she can improve.

> That was really good. I liked the anecdote you told and the slides you used were good. Next time, you could try using more evidence to support what you say.

10 Mind and machine

Neil Harbisson, a 'cyborg artist' who can only see in black and white, uses his antenna to 'hear' the colours around him

WARM UP

Look at the photo and read the caption. Discuss the questions.

1 How would you feel about having technology attached to your head?

2 How do you think you 'hear' colours?

3 If technology could improve one of your senses, which would you choose? Why?

In this unit you:

- talk about the functions of the human brain
- learn to use adverbial phrases
- watch a TED Talk by **TAN LE** about technology with life-changing applications

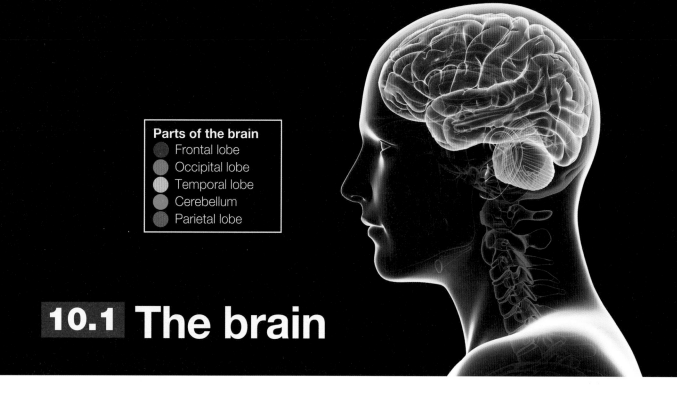

Parts of the brain
- Frontal lobe
- Occipital lobe
- Temporal lobe
- Cerebellum
- Parietal lobe

10.1 The brain

VOCABULARY Brain functions

1 ▶ 10.1 Listen and match each part of the brain with its function.

1 Frontal lobe	**a**	long-term **memory**, understanding language
2 Occipital lobe	**b**	pain and touch **sensations**, numbers, spelling
3 Temporal lobe	**c**	**concentration**, problem-solving, **emotions**
4 Cerebellum	**d**	processing visual information, **dreams**
5 Parietal lobe	**e**	**balance**, hand-eye coordination

2 Complete the sentences. Circle the correct words.

1 **Balance** is important when you *sleep / walk*.

2 When you **concentrate**, you *talk quickly / think hard* about something.

3 **Dreams** are events or images you experience in your mind when you're *asleep / awake*.

4 An example of an **emotion** is *love / language*.

5 Your **memory** is your ability to *create / remember* things.

6 A **sensation** is a *physical feeling / type of memory*.

3 Work in pairs. What part(s) of the brain are involved in these activities?

solving a maths problem	playing tennis	cooking dinner
looking at a pretty sunset	writing an essay	remembering your fifth birthday

I think solving a maths problem involves the frontal lobe.

I agree. I think it also involves the …

LISTENING The power of visualization

> **Listening for instructions**
> In English, instructions are often given using the imperative form of the verb. For example:
>
> Take notes.   Don't forget to ...   Be careful.

Brian Scholl

4 ▶ **10.2** Listen to psychology professor Brian Scholl describe a simple experiment. What is the aim of the experiment?

5 ▶ **10.2** Listen again. Number the steps in the experiment 1–4.

a Try to make some baskets. _____

b Crumple up some pieces of paper. _____

c Visualize your throw and then try to make some baskets. _____

d Set up a wastepaper basket. _____

Pronunciation Word stress with three-syllable words

6a ▶ **10.3** Listen to where the stress falls on these words.

Ooo	oOo
visualize	per**form**ance

6b ▶ **10.4** Add these words to the table. Listen and check. Then listen again and repeat.

concentrate   memory   physical   emotion   remember   sensation

SPEAKING Talking about a game

7 ▶ **10.5** Listen to the conversation. What kind of game is speaker B playing on their phone?

A: Hey, what are you doing?

B: I'm playing a brain game.

A: A brain game? What's that?

B: It's an app that exercises your brain. Do you want to **try**?   **have a go / give it a go**

A: **Yeah, OK.**   **Sure! / I'd love to!**

B: There are different games that exercise different parts of your brain.

A: Wow! This one's really **tricky**.   **complicated / difficult**

B: Yeah, it is at first. But **keep trying**. You'll get better really quickly.   **don't give up / try again**

8 Practise the conversation with a partner. Practise again using the words on the right.

9 Work in pairs. Try this brain game. Say the colour of each word. Do not read the word itself.

red blue green **black orange** blue **white yellow pink**

10 Was the game in Exercise 9 difficult? Why? Turn to page 158 and try two more brain games.

10.2 That's amazing!

THE INCREDIBLE BRAIN
Here are six amazing facts about our incredible brains.

We have an average of **70,000** thoughts every day.

The **100,000** miles of fibres that connect parts of the brain could easily circle the Earth four times.

Your brain can't feel **pain**.

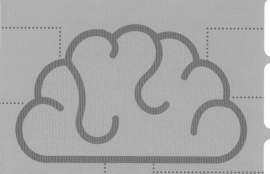

Your brain uses **20%** of the total oxygen in your body.

An average human brain has an estimated **100 billion** brain cells.

The **structure** of your brain changes every time you learn something new.

GRAMMAR Adverbs and adverbial phrases

1 ▶ **10.6** Look at the infographic. Which fact do you find the most incredible?

2 ▶ **10.7** Listen to an expert give more information about the brain. Circle **T** for true or **F** for false.

1 Your brain can generate enough energy to power a light bulb.　　　　**T**　　**F**

2 Humans only use about ten per cent of their brain.　　　　**T**　　**F**

3 Men's and women's brains are the same size.　　　　**T**　　**F**

3 ▶ **10.8** Read the sentences in the Grammar box. Answer the questions (a–d).

4 Put the words in the correct order to make sentences.

1 time / for / science / Randy / studied / a / long

_____

2 ten / age / three languages / of / Carrie / the / learned / before

_____

3 easily / word problems / Bianca / solve / can

_____

4 the exam / unfortunately / Matt / didn't pass

_____

ADVERBS AND ADVERBIAL PHRASES

Time	Other examples
We have an average of 70,000 thoughts **every day**. Your brain stops growing **at the age of 25**.	a day after a while
Manner	**Other examples**
Without oxygen, your brain would **quickly** die. The children are playing brain games **quietly**.	slowly calmly
Attitude	**Other examples**
Hopefully, tech innovations will help people with brain injuries. **Fortunately**, researchers are learning more and more about the brain.	Interestingly Luckily

Which kind of adverbs or adverbial phrases:

a usually go at the end of the sentence?
b go at the end or before the verb?

c go at the beginning of the sentence?
d are followed by a comma?

Check your answers on page 150 and do Exercises 1–2.

5 Complete the sentences. Circle the correct words.

1 We worked *very hard* / *hardly* to think of a solution.

2 He thought the answer was really *obvious* / *obviously*.

3 *Amazing* / *Amazingly*, he memorized all the words in the book.

4 He answered all the questions *correct* / *correctly*.

5 She's very *good* / *well* at doing maths in her head.

6 He was *lucky* / *luckily* to have such an amazing brain.

6 Complete each sentence with **two** of these time adverbials.

all day	at night
during the summer	next week
in a couple of hours	soon
in the morning	until I went to bed
in the university holidays	the day after tomorrow

1 I spent a week on a psychology course _____ / _____.

2 Sorry, I'm writing an essay this weekend. How about meeting _____ / _____?

3 I'm just taking Paul to work. I'll be back _____ / _____.

4 I usually concentrate best _____ / _____.

5 The sensation lasted _____ / _____.

Pronunciation Pausing with adverbs of attitude

7a ▶ 10.9 Listen to how we emphasize adverbs of attitude and pause after them.

1 Amazingly, my grandfather can still remember poems he learned at school.

2 Unfortunately, I wasn't very good at maths at college.

3 Interestingly, I couldn't do the brain game, but my younger brother could.

7b Write three sentences using adverbs of attitude. Practise saying your sentences. Remember to pause after the adverb.

8 ▶ 10.10 Complete the information with these words. One is extra. Listen and check your answers.

at	amazingly	constantly	easily
for	in	well	

Author Daniel Tammet is very good with numbers. [1]_____, he can memorize pi (π) to 22,500 digits, and he can multiply huge numbers in his head [2]_____ just seconds.

For Tammet, each number has a colour, shape and texture. He says the number 1 is like a shining light, 3 is green and 5 is like thunder.

This ability enables him to perform amazing feats quite [3]_____. As Tammet explains, 'When I multiply numbers together, I see two shapes. The image starts to change and evolve, and a third shape emerges.'

As a child, Tammet [4]_____ suffered from violent and painful seizures – sudden attacks that affect the heart and brain. In spite of this, he performed extremely [5]_____ at school. Tammet only discovered why he was different [6]_____ the age of 25. Doctors diagnosed him as being an autistic savant – a person with a developmental disorder who has extraordinary abilities.

Daniel Tammet can multiply huge numbers in his head

SPEAKING A logic puzzle

9 Work in pairs. You are going to try a logic puzzle. Turn to page 158 and follow the instructions.

10.3 Look, no hands!

READING The power of the mind

1 Look at the title and read the article quickly. What do you think the article is mainly about?

    a the problems of using mind-control technology

    b applications of mind-control technology

2 ▶ **10.11** Read the article. Check your prediction.

Understanding main ideas

3 Match the two parts to make sentences.

1 Thinker Thing	**a** allows someone to control a car using their mind.
2 The BrainDriver application	**b** makes music using people's thoughts.
3 The MiND Ensemble	**c** creates objects using mind control.

Understanding details

4 Complete the Venn diagram. Write the letters a–f.

    a uses an EEG headset

    b connects to a 3D printer

    c needs a computer

    d was developed in Europe

    e creates something new

    f shows objects on a screen

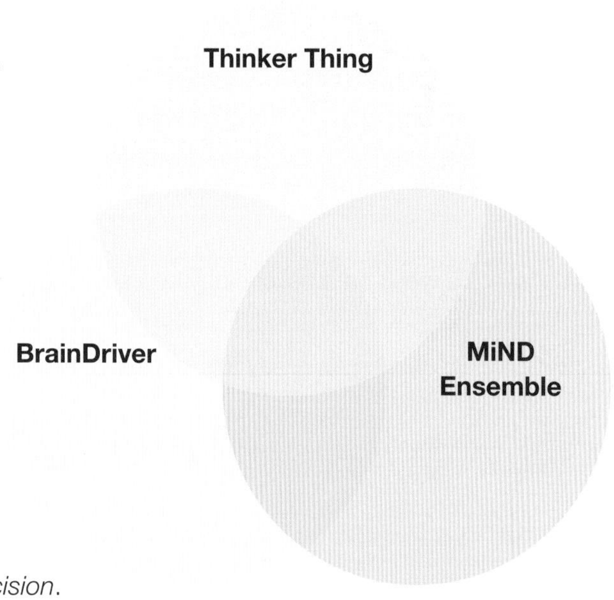

Thinker Thing

BrainDriver

MiND Ensemble

Understanding vocabulary

5 Circle the correct option to complete the sentences.

    1 A **breakthrough** is an important *discovery / decision*.

    2 If something **evolves**, it *stays the same / changes*.

    3 If something is **autonomous**, *no one / one person* controls it.

    4 If you **interpret** something, you work out the *cause / meaning* of it.

    5 A **signal** is a way of sending and receiving *information / objects*.

6 Work in pairs. Make a list of the advantages and disadvantages of each piece of technology mentioned in the article. Which of the applications do you think will be most common in the future?

A car is driven hands-free in a demonstration

THE POWER OF THE MIND

Mind control is no longer science fiction. Thanks to **breakthroughs** in our understanding of the brain, together with new technology, there are already some amazing things we can do.

5 Thinker Thing

In 2012, the Chilean company Thinker Thing was the first to create an object using only thoughts. The company used an [1]EEG headset, which records **signals** from the brain, together with a 10 3D printer, to show someone a series of **evolving** shapes on a computer screen. The EEG headset was able to tell if the user had positive or negative responses to the shapes. Eventually, an object was printed in 3D in response to the user's 15 [2]preferences. As this technology improves, it's possible that every child will be able to design and build their perfect toy in just minutes.

BrainDriver

In Germany, engineers have developed an 20 application called BrainDriver that allows a driver to control a car with his or her mind. The idea is to combine an EEG headset with an **autonomous** driving system. So as your car drives itself, you'll be able to make some [3]key decisions without pressing any buttons. For example, you'll be able to choose 25 a more interesting route, speed up or make a stop to pick up some food. All these decisions could be made using your mind and **interpreted** by the car's computer.

MiND Ensemble 30

At the University of Michigan, the MiND Ensemble (Music in Neural Dimensions) creates music based on a person's thoughts. A performer wears EEG headwear and special computer software then produces different sounds and musical notes based 35 on their brain signals. So, as the person's thoughts change, so does the music. Right now, [4]there is no guarantee that the music in your head will be the same as the music that the computer produces, but in the future, who knows? 40

---

[1] **EEG (acronym)** electroencephalography

[2] **preference (n)** something you like more than something else

[3] **key (adj)** very important

[4] **there is no guarantee (phrase)** it's not certain

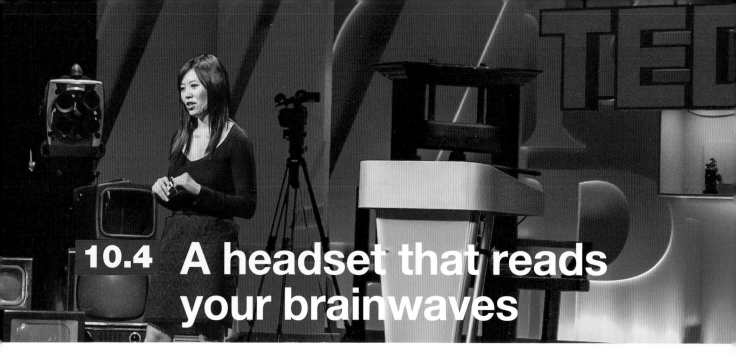

10.4 A headset that reads your brainwaves

TEDTALKS

1 Read the paragraph. Match each **bold** word with its meaning (1–4). You will hear these words in the TED Talk.

> In **TAN LE**'s talk, she demonstrates a new computer **interface** that makes it possible to control **virtual** objects simply by **visualizing** their movement. Her idea worth spreading is that new technology that 'reads our minds' has all kinds of life-changing **applications**, particularly for the disabled.

1 existing only on computers: _____

2 uses of an idea: _____

3 creating an image in the mind: _____

4 the connection between a human and a computer: _____

2 ▶ **10.12** Complete the summary with these words. Then watch Part 1 of the TED Talk to check your answers.

> body language   brain   emotions   human   light   machine

Human-to-¹_____ **communication**

- until now, limited to conscious and direct forms, e.g. turning on a ²_____
- people need to give a command to a machine to get it to do something

Human-to-³_____ **communication**

- more complex because we get information from facial expressions and ⁴_____
- can also understand feelings and ⁵_____ from talking to someone

Tan Le's goal

- to get computers to respond more like a person would by interpreting signals from the ⁶_____

3 ▶ **10.13** Watch Part 2 of the TED Talk. Number the steps in Tan Le's demonstration (1–5).

a Evan imagines an object coming forwards again. _____

b The computer learns how Evan thinks about 'pull'. _____

c Evan chooses to visualize the action 'pull'. _____

d Tan Le asks Evan to visualize the object coming forwards for eight seconds. _____

e The object moves forwards on the screen. _____

4 ▶ **10.14** Watch Part 3 of the TED Talk. What does Tan Le say the technology can be used for? Tick (✓) each thing she mentions.

a gaming   **c** driving cars   **e** controlling things in your house

b toys   **d** education   **f** helping people with disabilities

CRITICAL THINKING

5 Work in pairs. Think of five everyday tasks you would like to be able to perform using your mind. Would there be any disadvantages?

VOCABULARY IN CONTEXT

6 ▶ **10.15** Watch the clips from the TED Talk. Choose the correct meaning of the words.

7 Work in pairs. Complete the sentences in your own words.

  1 Controlling technology with your mind could be very useful. On the other hand ….

  2 The vision I have for my career is …

PRESENTATION SKILLS Dealing with the unexpected

Even with a well-prepared presentation, some things may go wrong or things may happen that the presenter did not expect. The best thing to do in these situations is to relax and calmly continue. Some things that are unexpected may be positive, such as when the audience is especially responsive to your ideas.

8 ▶ **10.16** Watch another part of Tan Le's TED Talk. What happened that was unexpected?

  a Evan couldn't think of a word.

  b Evan misunderstood the directions.

  c The demo didn't seem to work well.

9 ▶ **10.16** Watch the clip again. How did Tan Le deal with the unexpected?

10 Work in a group. What other unexpected things could happen during a presentation?

Well, you could forget what you wanted to say.

Or someone could interrupt you and ask a question.

10.5 It'll make your life easier

COMMUNICATE Creating a new product

1 Work in a group. Think about the technology that Tan Le described. Discuss some possible applications of the technology. Look at the these categories for ideas.

travel	shopping	sports	education
work	saving lives	disabilities	entertainment

2 Choose one application of Tan Le's technology and think of a new product that could make use of it. Prepare to explain what it does, how it's useful and who should buy it. Make notes.

> Name of product:
>
> What it does:
>
> How it's useful:
>
> Who should buy it:

EXPLAINING THE USES OF SOMETHING

It's useful for ...   You can use it to ...   It's designed for ...

3 Prepare a TV advertisement for your product. Write a short script. Then act out the advert for the class.

> Do you ever get hungry but feel too busy to make a snack?

> With Mind Delivery, you won't need to cook again. It works like this ...

WRITING Writing a proposal

4 Choose one of the products you heard about in Exercise 3. Write an email to Tan Le telling her about the product. Explain what it is and how it works.

> Dear Tan Le,
> I have a great idea for a product that uses your amazing new technology.
> If you're not too busy, I'd like to take some time to explain it to you ...

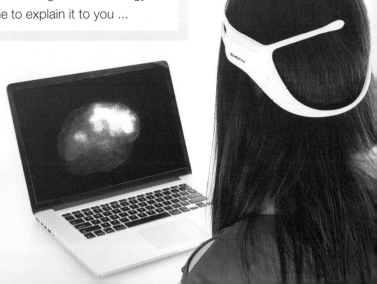

11 Nature

Millions of monarch butterflies make the
long journey south to Mexico every winter

WARM UP

Look at the photo and read the caption.
Discuss the questions.

1 What other extraordinary journeys do you know
of in the natural world?

2 Nature often provides memorable sights. Can you
think of any you've seen?

3 How do you enjoy spending time in nature?

In this unit you:

- talk about nature
- learn to use the present perfect
- watch a TED Talk by **LOUIE
  SCHWARTZBERG** about
  the wonder of pollination

11.1 Nature at its best

VOCABULARY Nature

1 Complete the table with these words. Can you add one more word to each column?

the coast	the desert	an island	a forest	the mountains	top of a mountain	the woods

on	in
the beach	a cave

2 Match the verbs and the activities. Try to add one more activity to each set.

1 go   **a** walk / bike ride

2 go for a   **b** diving / climbing / cycling / camping

3 go on   **c** safari / a walking holiday / a bike ride

3 Look at these words to describe a landscape or view. Are they positive (P) or neutral (N)? Can you think of places you would describe with these words?

1 wild _____   **4** gorgeous _____

2 breathtaking _____   **5** pretty _____

3 mountainous _____   **6** flat _____

4 How often do you spend time in the countryside? What do you like to do there? Discuss with a partner.

> I try to go out every week. I love walking.

> I go walking about once a month.

LISTENING My experiences in nature

> **Noticing auxiliary verbs**
> Auxiliary verbs are often contracted and can be difficult to hear. Being able to recognize different auxiliary verbs will help you understand a speaker's message. For example, *I have* is usually shortened to *I've*.

5 ▶ **11.1** Listen to Tony Gainsford talking about his experiences in nature. Circle the natural places that he can enjoy near his home.

> a beach   a forest   a park   a river

6 ▶ **11.1** Listen again. Match the sentence parts to make statements about Gainsford's experiences.

1 He's been snorkelling in   **a** Africa.
2 He saw sea turtles in   **b** Australia.
3 He's never been to   **c** Greece.

7 Have you had any similar experiences to Gainsford? Discuss with a partner.

Tony Gainsford

Pronunciation /ðə/ and /ði:/

8a ▶ **11.2** Listen to the different way *the* is pronounced before a consonant sound and before a vowel sound.

there's a great park along **the** coast here
female turtles come to **the** island's beaches

8b ▶ **11.3** Listen and repeat.

1 the coast   **2** the island   **3** the Arctic   **4** the desert   **5** the wildlife   **6** the Earth

SPEAKING Talking about nature

9 ▶ **11.4** Listen to the conversation. Where are the two people planning to go?

A: It's great to get out and **enjoy** the countryside while the weather is so nice.   appreciate / experience

B: You know, we should go to Evans National Forest sometime.

A: That would be fun. I've never been there. Have you?

B: Yeah, I have. It was **so pretty**.   breathtaking / gorgeous

A: Have you ever **walked up** the mountain there?   climbed up / been to the top of

B: No, I haven't. I'd love to, though.

A: OK, we should make a plan. Hopefully, we'll **spot** some deer or other wildlife.   see / find

10 Practise the conversation with a partner. Practise again using the words on the right.

11 Work in pairs. Think of something fun to do outside together.

> What do you think we should do?

> How about going for a walk by the river? It's really nice.

11.2 Have you ever seen a bear?

DISCONNECTED FROM NATURE

More and more children today are having less and less contact with the natural world. A recent survey of 2,000 British children between the ages of 8 and 12 had some surprising results.

20% have never climbed a tree.

21% have never visited a farm.

40% have never been camping.

28% have not been on a walk in the countryside in the last year.

Only **36%** have played outside in the last week.

More go to hospital from falling out of bed than from falling out of a tree.

GRAMMAR Present perfect

1 ▶ **11.5** Look at the infographic. Do you think children in your country are similar? Discuss with a partner.

2 ▶ **11.6** Listen to a health expert offer some advice. Complete the suggestions.

1 Adults need to _____ for children.

2 We need to look at why children are _____ more.

3 For a few hours a week, parents shouldn't allow their children to _____.

3 Read the sentences in the Grammar box. Answer the questions (a–d).

PRESENT PERFECT

1 I've **been** camping.

2 I **went** when I was ten.

3 She **has**n't **visited** a farm.

a Which sentence describes an event that happened sometime in the past (but we don't know exactly when)?

b Which sentence describes an event that happened at a definite time in the past?

c How do we form the present perfect, and how do we make it negative?

d What is the main verb in sentence 1? *Go* or *be*?

Check your answers on page 152 and do Exercises 1–2.

---

4 Complete the text with the present perfect form of the verbs. Use contractions where possible.

Pippa Hawkins teaches pre-school children. She says that many of the children in her class ¹ *have never run* (never run) in the countryside and often, they ² _____ (not hear) the sound a cow makes except on TV! But Pippa has started to change this. 'I ³ _____ (take) them to the woods and we ⁴ _____ (go) on a trip to a local river, too.' Now a child can go home and say that he ⁵ _____ (climb) a tree, or that she ⁶ _____ (see) a big fish.

Pippa says, 'They ⁷ _____ (learn) a lot about nature and I ⁸ _____ (enjoy) seeing how happy being outdoors makes the children.' Perhaps this is a lesson that we can all learn from.

LANGUAGE FOCUS Talking about past experiences

5 ▶ **11.7** Study the examples in the Language focus box.

TALKING ABOUT PAST EXPERIENCES

Have you **ever climbed** a tree?	Yes, I **have**. I**'ve climbed** lots of trees. Yes, but I **haven't climbed** one since I was a child.
Has she **ever slept** outdoors?	Yes, she **has**. She**'s been** camping twice. No, she **hasn't**. She**'s never slept** outdoors.
Have you **ever been** to a desert?	Yes, I **have**. I went to one in Chile last year. No, but I'd like to.
I**'ve had** a walk every day this week.	Me too. / So **have** I. Really? I **haven't**.
I**'ve never swum** in the sea.	Me neither. / I **haven't**, either. / Neither **have** I. Really? I **have**.

For more information and practice, go to page 152.

6 ▶ **11.8** Complete the information with the correct form of these verbs. Listen and check your answers.

build	connect	love
make	~~see~~	want

Have you ever ¹ ___seen___ a tree house?
Have you ever ² _____ to live in one? One man has ³ _____ that dream come true.

Foster Huntington has always ⁴ _____ tree houses, and when he decided to move from New York City to Oregon he had an idea: he would build his own.

He has ⁵ _____ not one, but two tree houses. And he has ⁶ _____ them with a bridge to create a truly unique living space high above the ground. It may not be for everyone, but for Huntington, it's the perfect home.

Foster Huntington and his treehouse

7 Complete the conversations.

1 A: Have you ever been camping?
   B: Yes, I *did / have*. I *went / have been* camping last summer.
2 A: *Has / Have* you ever *swam / swum* in the sea?
   B: No, I haven't. But I *swam / 've swum* in a river last summer.
3 A: *Did you see / Have you seen* any bears on your trip last August?
   B: No, but my brother *saw / has seen* one a couple of years ago.

Pronunciation Weak forms (2): *have*

8 ▶ **11.9** Listen to how *have* is pronounced in these examples. Listen again and repeat.

1 **Have** you ever been sailing?
2 Yes, I **have**.
3 No, I **have**n't. But I**'ve** been on a canal boat.

SPEAKING Experiences in nature

9 Walk around the classroom. Find someone who answers *yes* to each question. Then ask a follow-up question.

Have you ever …

- climbed a tree?
- been camping?
- been diving?
- visited a farm?
- planted a tree?

Have you ever planted a tree?

Yes, I have.

Where did you plant it?

11.3 Small is beautiful

READING The miracle of pollen

1 Read the definition of *pollen* in the glossary on page 121. What animals do you know that help carry pollen? Discuss with a partner.

2 ▶ **11.10** Read the article. Which animals are mentioned?

Understanding gist

3 Choose the best alternative title for the article.

   a The secret life of bees   **b** The importance of pollinators   **c** The wonder of reproduction

Understanding a process

4 How does pollination work? Complete the information using these words.

body	nectar	petals	pollen	seed

- A flower with bright ¹_____ and a sweet smell attracts a bee.

- The bee lands on the flower and drinks its ²_____ .

- Some pollen gets on the bee's ³_____ .

- The bee lands on another flower and deposits the ⁴_____ there.

- The flower now has what it needs to produce a ⁵_____ , which will grow into a new plant.

Understanding details

5 Circle **T** for true or **F** for false.

  1 If pollination stopped, there would be no tomatoes.   **T**   **F**

  2 There are over 200,000 different types of pollinators.   **T**   **F**

  3 Ants are the only non-flying pollinators.   **T**   **F**

  4 Today, there are more honey bees in the United States than ever before.   **T**   **F**

  5 Scientists have discovered the reason for colony collapse disorder.   **T**   **F**

Understanding vocabulary

6 Circle the correct words to complete the definitions.

  1 If something **attracts** you, you want to be *closer to / further away from* it.

  2 If you **tear** something **open**, you open it by *pulling with your hands / using a knife*.

  3 If you **depend on** something, you *need / don't need* it.

  4 A **serious** problem is *big / small*.

  5 If something **disappears**, you can't *see / understand* it anymore.

7 What could be done to protect pollinating plants? Discuss with a partner.

A bee collects pollen from a lily flower

THE MIRACLE OF POLLEN

It happens countless times a day. A flower's bright petals and the smell of sweet [1]nectar **attract** a bee. The bee drops in for a quick taste, and small [2]grains of [3]pollen stick to its body. The
5 bee then travels to another flower of the same type and as it stops for another meal, leaves the pollen. This is an example of animal pollination – a process vital to plant [4] reproduction.

It's not only plants that **depend on** animal
10 pollination – humans do, too. Worldwide, approximately a thousand plants that we grow for food, spices, clothing and medicine depend on it. If pollination suddenly stopped, we would have no more apples, tomatoes or coffee and it would be
15 the end of many other products, too.

This essential process is carried out by more than 200,000 different animal species known as pollinators. Flies and beetles – the original pollinators – have performed this task for 130 million
20 years, since the time of the first flowering plants. Birds, butterflies and ants also do their part. Even non-flying mammals help out: monkeys **tear open** flowers with their hands, accidentally spreading pollen into the air and onto their fur.

However, some of our most important pollinators 25 are at risk. Climate change, habitat loss and invasive predators all threaten them. The United States, for example, has lost over 50 per cent of its honeybees over the past ten years. A **serious** threat facing bees is colony collapse 30 disorder (CCD), when worker bees mysteriously **disappear** from their colony. Scientists are still trying to identify its cause.

There is a quote [5]attributed to Einstein that says if bees disappeared, man would only have four 35 years left to live. Whether that's true or not does not really matter, says wildlife photographer Louie Schwartzberg: the key point is that there is a real danger. 'We depend on pollinators for over a third of the fruits and vegetables we eat', he says. And 40 this food 'would disappear without pollinating plants. It's pretty serious.'

---

[1] **nectar (n)** a sweet liquid produced by flowers

[2] **grain (n)** a piece of something (e.g. salt, sand) that is very small

[3] **pollen (n)** very fine, usually yellow, powder that is produced by a plant. It is carried to other plants of the same kind so that the plants can produce seeds.

[4] **reproduction (n)** the process by which living things produce young

[5] **attributed to (phrase)** believed to be said by a particular person

121

Louie Schwartzberg

11.4 The hidden beauty of pollination

TEDTALKS

1 Read the paragraph. Complete the definitions (1–3). You will hear these words in the TED Talk.

> As a filmmaker, **LOUIE SCHWARTZBERG** uses **time-lapse** photography and slow-motion cameras to capture amazing images of nature. He is fascinated by the way plants and pollinators **co-evolve** and believes that threats to pollinators deserve our attention. His idea worth spreading is that we will protect what we fall in love with, so we should enjoy the beauty in nature and **take care of** it.

   1 **Time-lapse** photography makes a *slow action appear fast / fast action appear slow*.

   2 If two or more species **co-evolve**, they develop particular features *separately / together*.

   3 You **take care of** something that is *important / unimportant* to you.

2 ▶ **11.11** Watch Part 1 of the TED Talk. Choose the correct options to complete the summary.

Louie Schwartzberg thinks the [1]*little things / big ideas* in life are the most amazing. He describes how pollinators and flowers co-evolved over a period of [2]*50 / 15* million years. He describes watching flowers with time-lapse photography as a kind of [3]*magic / dance*. He wants to take action to protect the [4]*bees / flowers* because if they disappear, we do too.

3 ▶ **11.12** Watch Part 2 of the TED Talk. What do you think Louie Schwartzberg means by each statement?

   1 'So here is some nectar from my film.'

   a Here are the parts that include flowers.

   b Here are some of the best parts of my film.

   2 'I hope you'll drink, tweet and plant some seeds to pollinate a friendly garden.'

   a I hope you enjoy it and share it with others.

   b I hope you get inspired to plant your own garden.

   3 'And always take time to smell the flowers, and let it fill you with beauty ...'

   a Take the time to appreciate the beautiful and natural things in life.

   b When you buy flowers, remember to choose the most beautiful ones.

CREATIVE THINKING

4 What other things would be interesting to film with time-lapse photography? Discuss with a partner.

VOCABULARY IN CONTEXT

5 ▶ **11.13** Watch the clips from the TED Talk. Choose the correct meaning of the words.

6 Work in pairs. Discuss the questions.

1 Are there any causes you care about enough to take action?

2 Are there any books you love and have read over and over again?

PRESENTATION SKILLS Calling others to action

TIPS

One effective way of closing a presentation is with a call to action — when the presenter calls upon the audience to act in some way. Often the presenter uses *we* or *our* to stress that we are all part of the solution.

7 ▶ **11.14** Watch the clip. Notice how Louie Schwartzberg says 'we need' to take care of nature.

8 ▶ **11.15** Can you remember what these TED speakers' calls to action were? Match. Then watch the clips and check your answers.

1 Munir Virani

a 'And I hope many more people will join me. If we all read more widely, there'd be more incentive for publishers to …'

2 Ann Morgan

b 'It is up to us to decide whether we want schools or parking lots, community-driven recycling projects, or …'

3 Andras Forgacs

c 'You can write a letter to your government and tell them that we need to focus on these very misunderstood creatures.'

4 Alessandra Orofino

d 'We can design new materials, new products and new facilities. We need to move past just killing animals …'

9 Work in a group. What are some things that you think Schwartzberg would like to see people do to 'take care of nature'?

A hummingbird feeds on the nectar of a flower, Costa Rica

123

11.5 Getting out into nature

COMMUNICATE Planning a weekend in the countryside

1 Work in a group. You're going to plan a weekend camping trip in the countryside. Decide on a suitable place to go camping. Explain why this is a good place.

2 Work together to think of six possible activities to do during the weekend. The aim is to have new experiences and learn about the natural world. Include activities that your group members have never done before.

Activities

Day 1

1 _____
2 _____
3 _____

Day 2

1 _____
2 _____
3 _____

> Have you ever been canoeing?

> No, I haven't. That's a good idea. Let's do that.

3 Join another group. Explain your plan. Answer any questions they may have.

ASKING FOR MORE DETAILS

What exactly …?   What kind of …?   Can you explain why you …?

WRITING Writing a journal entry

4 Imagine the first day of your weekend in the countryside has just ended. Write a journal entry describing your experiences and your planned activities for tomorrow.

> My weekend in the countryside is going really well! So far, I've planted a tree, made a campfire using sticks and been bird watching. I've had such a great time. Tomorrow will be fun as well. In the morning, we're going to …

12 Discovery

A scientist explores an ice cave on Ross Island, Antarctica

WARM UP

Look at the photo and read the caption. Discuss the questions.

1 If you found a cave, would you explore it?

2 Have you ever found anything interesting while out walking?

3 Can you think of any recent discoveries that have taught us more about the past?

In this unit you:

- talk about discoveries
- learn to use the passive
- watch a TED Talk by **NIZAR IBRAHIM** about some amazing dinosaur discoveries

An artefact from the fifth century BC discovered in Lavau, France

12.1 Recent discoveries

VOCABULARY Discoveries

1 Look at the photo and read the information. Match each **bold** word with its meaning (1–3).

In 2015, archaeologists **discovered** a tomb from the fifth century BC that is thought to belong to a Celtic prince. After **excavating** the site in Lavau, France and **inspecting** the contents of the tomb, a number of high-quality artefacts were found.

1 digging up: _____   **2** found: _____   **3** looking at: _____

2 Complete the sentences with these words.

> fossil   ruins   pottery   tomb   artefacts

1 The _____ of an ancient city were identified from the air.

2 Tutankhamun's _____ contained piles of gold.

3 The _____ of a five-centimetre-long ant was discovered in 2011.

4 Researchers believe the pieces of _____ were once large jars that held oil.

5 A number of valuable _____, including several gold vases, were also found.

3 Think of a museum or historical site you have visited. What did you see there? Discuss with a partner.

I visited the British Museum in London a few years ago. They have a lot of artefacts from ancient Egypt. It was really interesting.

LISTENING An amazing find

> **Listening for numbers and dates**
> It's a good idea to practise saying numbers out loud so you are familiar with how they sound. It's also useful to learn the different ways we say dates.
>
> | | |
> |---|---|
> | 5 March | March the fifth / the fifth of March |
> | 2014 | two thousand and fourteen / twenty fourteen |

4 ▶ **12.1** Listen to archaeologist Fredrik Hiebert talking about a discovery he made. What artefact did he find? Circle the correct answer.

Fredrik Hiebert

a door   a key   a crown   a ring

5 ▶ **12.1** Listen again. Complete the table.

Where was the site?	How old was the artefact?	Who did the artefact belong to?
on the coast of ¹_____	over ²_____ years old	a merchant who only lived there in ³_____

6 What can we learn about the past from Fredrik Hiebert's discovery? Discuss with a partner.

Pronunciation Numbers and dates

7 ▶ **12.2** Work in pairs. Can you pronounce these numbers and dates? Listen and check. Then listen again and repeat.

1 1,000 years old   **3** in 1784   **5** on 14 September

2 1,500 years ago   **4** in 2018   **6** a 40-year-old man

SPEAKING Talking about a discovery

8 ▶ **12.3** Listen to the conversation. How did the archaeologists find the site?

A: Wow! This is interesting. **Apparently,** archaeologists have found an ancient lost city in Honduras.   **According to this, / It says here that**

B: Really? How old is it?

A: Well, the artefacts they found there are **around** a thousand years old.   **about / approximately**

B: Wow! How did they find it?

A: The site was **identified** from the air. A team of archaeologists was **looking for** a city known as the 'City of the Monkey God'. They think this is it.   **discovered / located**   **searching for / trying to find**

B: How exciting!

9 Practise the conversation with a partner. Practise again using the words on the right.

10 What famous discoveries can you name? They can be in any field, such as archaeology, medicine, exploration or history.

> I heard that some scientists think they have discovered a new planet in our solar system.

> I heard about that too.

12.2 Amazing finds

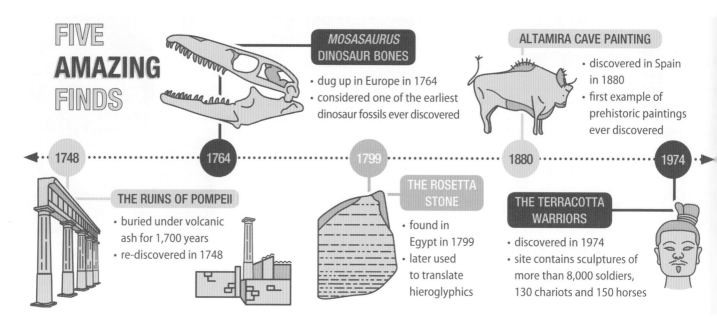

FIVE AMAZING FINDS

MOSASAURUS DINOSAUR BONES
- dug up in Europe in 1764
- considered one of the earliest dinosaur fossils ever discovered

ALTAMIRA CAVE PAINTING
- discovered in Spain in 1880
- first example of prehistoric paintings ever discovered

1748 ···· 1764 ···· 1799 ···· 1880 ···· 1974

THE RUINS OF POMPEII
- buried under volcanic ash for 1,700 years
- re-discovered in 1748

THE ROSETTA STONE
- found in Egypt in 1799
- later used to translate hieroglyphics

THE TERRACOTTA WARRIORS
- discovered in 1974
- site contains sculptures of more than 8,000 soldiers, 130 chariots and 150 horses

GRAMMAR The passive

1 ▶ 12.4 Look at the infographic. Which discovery do you think is the most interesting? Why?

2 ▶ 12.5 Listen to an expert talking about the terracotta warriors. Complete the sentences.

  1 The site was a _____ built for the first emperor of China.

  2 The site is over _____ years old.

  3 The sculptures were originally painted in _____ colours.

3 Read the sentences in the Grammar box. Answer the questions (a–e).

4 Complete the passive forms in the text with the correct past participles of the verbs.

The earliest cave paintings were [1]_____ (discover) in a cave called El Castillo in Northern Spain in 1903. Some images of hands were [2]_____ (reveal) that were [3]_____ (paint) nearly 40,000 years ago.

Until a few years ago, all early cave painting was [4]_____ (believe) to be in Europe. But in the 1950s, twelve images of hands and animals were [5]_____ (find) on the island of Sulawesi in Indonesia. The paintings were [6]_____ (study) in 2014 and were shown to be nearly 40,000 years old, about 30,000 years older than people thought.

THE PASSIVE

1 Thousands of people **visit** the sculptures every year.

2 The sculptures **are visited** by thousands of people every year.

3 The terracotta warriors **were discovered** in 1974.

a Is sentence 1 active or passive?

b Are sentences 2 and 3 active or passive?

c How do we change an active sentence into a passive sentence?

d In sentence 2, what word do we use before the agent (the person who performs the action)?

e Why might we prefer to use the passive in sentence 3?

Check your answers on page 153 and do Exercises 1–2.

LANGUAGE FOCUS Talking about discoveries

5 ▶ 12.6 Study the examples in the Language focus box.

TALKING ABOUT DISCOVERIES

Lots of tourists **visit** Pompeii.	Pompeii **is visited by** lots of tourists.
The museum **displays** many artefacts.	Many artefacts **are displayed by** the museum.
The volcanic ash **killed** people instantly.	People **were killed** instantly **by** the volcanic ash.
People **forgot** about the city.	The city **was forgotten** about.
Archaeologists **didn't discover** it until 1,700 years later.	It **wasn't discovered** until 1,700 years later.
Is the cave **protected**?	Yes, it **is**.
Are the walls **covered** in paintings?	Yes, they **are**.
Was the cave **found** recently?	No, it **wasn't**. It **was found** over 100 years ago.
Were the animals **painted** in colour?	Yes, they **were**.

For more information and practice, go to page 154.

Pronunciation Irregular past participles

6 ▶ 12.7 Write the past participle of these verbs (1–5 and a–e). Then match the past participles that have the same vowel sound. Listen and check. Listen again and repeat.

1 become *become*
2 build _____
3 buy _____
4 hear _____
5 read _____

a hurt _____
b sing *sung*
c say _____
d teach _____
e write _____

7 ▶ 12.8 Complete the information. Circle the correct options. Listen and check your answers.

The Voynich manuscript is one of the world's most mysterious books. The text ¹*writes / is written* from left to right and most pages have illustrations. The language used in the book is not known. Its alphabet ²*contains / is contained* 20–25 individual characters, and most of these ³*made / are made* using just one or two pen strokes.

Wilfrid Voynich – a Polish book dealer – ⁴*discovered / was discovered* the book in 1912, and it ⁵*names / is named* after him. Carbon dating shows that it ⁶*created / was created* in the early 15th century.

People have many questions about the manuscript. Some claim a microscope ⁷*needed / was needed* to draw some of the illustrations, but the microscope ⁸*didn't invent / wasn't invented* until the 16th century. Others say the dating is not accurate and argue that it's a modern fake.

8 Complete the conversations with the correct form of the verbs.

1 A: Who _____ (discover) the first dinosaur fossil?
   B: I'm not sure, but I think it _____ (find) in Europe somewhere.

2 A: Where _____ the Rosetta Stone _____ (locate) today?
   B: In the British Museum. It _____ (see) by 2.5 million people a year.

3 A: _____ King Tut _____ (bury) with a lot of valuable objects?
   B: Yes. After his tomb was opened, everything _____ (remove) and placed in a museum.

SPEAKING Discovery quiz

9 Work in pairs. You are going to do a quiz. Student A: turn to page 157. Student B: turn to page 159.

12.3 It's in his bones

READING The dinosaur hunter

1 Read the introduction to the interview. Think of three questions you'd like to ask Nizar Ibrahim.

2 ▶ 12.9 Read the interview. Which of your questions were answered?

Understanding gist

3 Tick (✓) the topics that are discussed in the interview.

    a why Nizar Ibrahim became a palaeontologist   **c** extreme weather Ibrahim has faced

    b an experience Ibrahim found thrilling   **d** advice Ibrahim received as a child

Understanding details

4 Are the following statements true, false or not given according to the interview?
Circle **T** for true, **F** for false or **NG** for not given.

    1 Ibrahim was interested in animals from a young age.   **T**   **F**   **NG**

    2 Ibrahim's uncle was a palaeontologist.   **T**   **F**   **NG**

    3 Ibrahim decided he wanted to be a palaeontologist
    when he was a teenager.   **T**   **F**   **NG**

    4 Ibrahim found a huge dinosaur bone in Morocco.   **T**   **F**   **NG**

    5 Ibrahim made an amazing discovery in the Sahara.   **T**   **F**   **NG**

Understanding pronoun referencing

5 Read the excerpts from the interview. What do the pronouns in **bold** refer to?

    1 '… **it** inspired me to want to write a book of my own.'
      a   receiving a book about dinosaurs   b meeting a famous author

    2 'I … added the word *Dr* in front of **it**.'
      a   the author's name   b his own name

    3 '… don't let anyone take **them** away from you.'
      a   your discoveries   b your dreams

    4 '… **which** turned out to be one of the most challenging trips.'
      a   a trip to Morocco   b a trip to the Sahara

Understanding vocabulary

6 Complete each sentence with a **bold** word from the interview.

    1 If you feel less determined or confident about something, you feel _____ .

    2 A(n) _____ storm is one that is strong and powerful.

    3 A person with very _____ interests is interested in many different things.

    4 _____ are difficulties that makes it hard to do something.

    5 A(n) _____ is a gradual increase in something.

7 What do you think is the most challenging aspect of being a palaeontologist? Discuss.

THE DINOSAUR HUNTER

Like many children, [1]palaeontologist Nizar Ibrahim had a fascination with dinosaurs. He has spent most of his life searching for their fossils.

5 What inspired you to dedicate your life to your work?

As a child, I was always interested in animals. I was five when I received my first book about dinosaurs, and it inspired me to want to write 10 a book of my own. When I was told that I would have to study hard and get a PhD, I wrote my name under the author's and added the word *Dr* in front of it. I made the decision then and there that I would become 15 a palaeontologist.

I am so inspired by the history of life on our planet. And I feel that palaeontology is our best tool to understand it.

What has been your most memorable 20 experience in the field?

It is difficult to choose one particular [2]memorable experience. Locating and unearthing the largest dinosaur bone ever found in the Kem Kem region of south-eastern Morocco was a thrilling experience.

There is a real **build-up** of excitement when 25 searching for fossils because most finds begin as small bits of bone, and the element of discovery and surprise is [3]ever-present.

What about the challenges?

The challenges I face during my [4]fieldwork are 30 very **diverse** and range from **violent** sandstorms and extensive flooding to working in the middle of the Sahara in 50°C heat.

Several years ago, I led a small expedition to the Sahara, on a very [5]restrictive budget, with just 35 one vehicle and extremely limited supplies, which turned out to be one of the most challenging trips.

What advice would you give your younger self?

First: follow your dreams and don't let anyone take them away from you. Second: don't be 40 **discouraged**. Hurdles and **obstacles** are a part of life and can be overcome. Third: make big plans.

---

[1] **palaeontologist (n)** a scientist who studies fossils
[2] **memorable (adj)** special and worth remembering
[3] **ever-present (adj)** constant, always there
[4] **fieldwork (n)** practical work done in the natural environment, not in an office or lab
[5] **restrictive (adj)** stopping someone from doing what they want to do

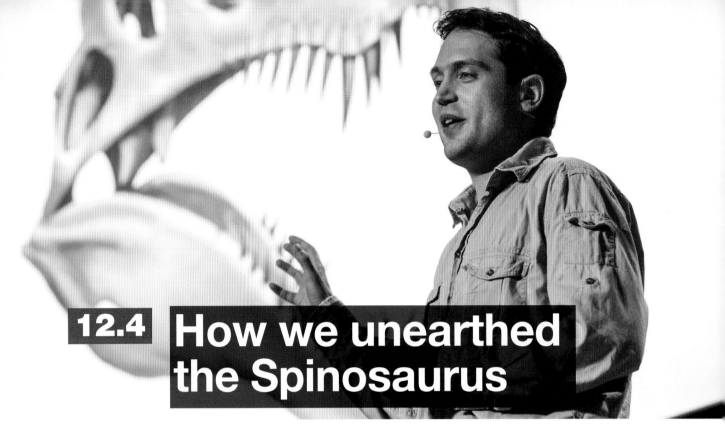

12.4 How we unearthed the Spinosaurus

TEDTALKS

1 Read the paragraph. Complete the definitions (1–3). You will hear these words in the TED Talk.

> **NIZAR IBRAHIM**'s **quest** to find dinosaur fossils has taken him to extreme corners of the planet. In the Sahara, he discovered the **remains** of a **bizarre** but beautiful creature. His idea worth spreading is that there will always be amazing discoveries and adventures for palaeontologists, archaeologists and other explorers.

1 A **quest** is *an unexpected discovery / a long search for something*.

2 The **remains** of a dinosaur might include its *bones / footprints*.

3 Something that is **bizarre** is very *difficult to find / strange or unusual*.

2 Look at the dinosaur on page 133. What can you learn about it from the illustration?

3 ▶ 12.10 Watch Part 1 of the TED Talk. What did Nazir Ibrahim already know about the Spinosaurus? Complete the notes.

- Some ¹_____ were discovered 100 years ago in Egypt but were destroyed in World War II.
- The Spinosaurus lived about ²_____ years ago.
- From drawings, we know it was big, had a sail on its ³_____ and a long jaw like a ⁴_____ .
- It probably ate ⁵_____ .

4 ▶ 12.11 Watch Part 2 of the TED Talk. What did Ibrahim discover about the Spinosaurus from the bones that were found? Circle the correct words.

1 The Spinosaurus's head was very *different from / similar to* other predatory dinosaurs.

2 The Spinosaurus's feet were similar in appearance to those of a *land / water* animal.

3 The structure of the Spinosaurus's bones suggests it spent a lot of time *walking / in the water*.

4 The Spinosaurus was *bigger / smaller* than a T. rex.

5 ▶ **12.12** Watch Part 3 of the TED Talk. Ibrahim quotes dinosaur hunter Roy Chapman Andrews when he says, 'Always, there has been an adventure just around the corner – and the world is still full of corners.' What does he mean by this?

CRITICAL THINKING

6 What kind of things do you think we will never know about the Spinosaurus? Why not? Discuss with a partner.

VOCABULARY IN CONTEXT

7 ▶ **12.13** Watch the clips from the TED Talk. Choose the correct meaning of the words.

8 Work in pairs. Complete the sentences in your own words.

    1 An example of a once-in-a-lifetime event is ….

    2 I find it sad that there are not many … left in the world.

PRESENTATION SKILLS Using descriptive language

A good presenter uses descriptive language to 'paint a picture'. One way to do this is to compare something to another thing the audience already knows so that it's easier to imagine.

9 ▶ **12.14** Watch the clip. Notice the descriptive language Nizar Ibrahim uses. Which animal does he compare the Spinosaurus's head to?

10 ▶ **12.15** Now watch three other TED speakers. Complete the sentences.

    1 Jarrett J. Krosoczka says a two-year-old's birthday cake is like a _____ .

    2 Munir Virani says that vultures are our natural _____ collectors.

    3 Louie Schwartzberg compares footage of time-lapse flowers to a _____ .

11 Work in pairs. Describe the picture on page 123. Use descriptive language.

The Spinosaurus hunting for food

12.5 What have you found?

COMMUNICATE A newspaper interview

1 Work in pairs. Read the information, then do the roleplay.

Student A: You are an archaeologist. Turn to page 159.
Student B: You are a newspaper reporter. Student A recently found some unusual items in the ground. You are going to interview him or her about the discovery. Prepare questions to ask.
- What?
- Where?
- When?
- How old?
- Importance?

EXPLAINING POSSİBILITIES

It's possible that ...   It could be that ...   There's a possibility that ...

2 Switch roles. Student B: Turn to page 160. Student A: Prepare questions to ask.

WRITING Reporting the news

3 Use the information you learned in Exercises 1 and 2 to write a short news report.

A mysterious skull was discovered last weekend in the garden of a local family. Lisa Morgan, a student at Mason College, was planting a tree behind her house when she made the discovery.

4 You are about to go on live TV to report your story. Read your news report to a partner.

MODEL PRESENTATION

1 Complete the transcript of the presentation using these words.

amazingly	discovered	forests	fossils	has been
have been	has eaten	hopefully	was created	was made

Today, I want to tell you about an amazing discovery that ¹_____
not so long ago. Take a look at this picture. This is Hang Son Doong – the
world's largest cave. I first heard about this place when I saw an unbelievable video
of it on YouTube. Hang Son Doong is in Vietnam. Its name means 'Mountain River
Cave'. How big is it? Well, it's more than 5 kilometres long, 200 metres
high and 150 metres wide. In some places the cave is big enough to fit a
jumbo jet inside! The cave ²_____ by a river which
³_____ away the limestone of the Annamite Mountains. How
was it ⁴_____? Well, ⁵_____, nobody knew
about this place until a local man named Ho Khanh found it by accident in
1991. And it was only in 2009 that the cave became internationally known after
a group of British scientists went there to study it. Inside the cave, entire
⁶_____ stretch out across the cave floor, and 300-million-
year-old ⁷_____ have been found inside. The cave is so large
it even has its own weather system. Very few people ⁸_____
inside the cave although it ⁹_____ open to the public since 2013.
¹⁰_____, I'll get the chance to go there myself one day. It looks like a truly
incredible place.

2 ▶ **P.4** Watch the presentation and check your answers.

3 ▶ **P.4** Review the list of presentation skills from units 1–12 below. Which does the
speaker use? Tick (✓) each skill used as you watch again.

Presentation skills: units 1–12			
The speaker …			
• uses questions to signpost	☐	• tells an anecdote	☐
• personalizes the presentation	☐	• uses supporting evidence	☐
• closes the presentation effectively	☐	• uses an effective slide	☐
• provides background information	☐	• uses descriptive language	☐
• numbers key points	☐	• gives a call to action	☐
• uses their voice effectively	☐	• deals with the unexpected	☐

YOUR TURN

4 You are going to plan and give a short presentation to a partner about an amazing discovery. Do research and make notes using some or all of the questions below.

> • What was the discovery?
> • Where was it discovered?
> • How was it discovered?
> • What did people learn from it?

5 Look at the Useful phrases box. Think about which ones you will need in your presentation.

USEFUL PHRASES

Discoveries	Places in nature
fossil, ruins, pottery, tomb, artefacts find, discover, excavate, inspect	river, cave, volcano, island, forest

Adverbial phrases	Talking about findings
amazingly, incredibly, unexpectedly	We now know that ... / It was discovered that ... We can now be sure that ...

6 Work in pairs. Take turns giving your presentation using your notes. Use some of the presentation skills from units 1–12. As you listen, tick (✓) each skill your partner uses.

Presentation skills: units 1–12			
The speaker ...			
• uses questions to signpost	☐	• tells an anecdote	☐
• personalizes the presentation	☐	• uses supporting evidence	☐
• closes the presentation effectively	☐	• uses an effective slide	☐
• provides background information	☐	• uses descriptive language	☐
• numbers key points	☐	• gives a call to action	☐
• uses their voice effectively	☐	• deals with the unexpected	☐

7 Give your partner some feedback on their talk. Include two things you liked, and one thing he or she can improve.

> Well done! You used some great descriptive language and I thought you used evidence well. Next time, try to provide a bit more background information.

GRAMMAR Present simple and present continuous

Form

Present simple

Affirmative	Negative
I/You/We/They **help**.	I/You/We/They **don't help**. (don't = do not)
He/She/It **helps**.	He/She/It **doesn't help**. (doesn't = does not)

Question	Short answer
Do I/you/we/they **help**?	Yes, you/I/we/they **do**. No, you/I/we/they **don't**.
Does he/she/it **help**?	Yes, he/she/it **does**. No, he/she/it **doesn't**.

Present continuous

Affirmative	Negative
I**'m helping**. ('m = am)	I**'m not helping**. ('m not = am not)
You**'re**/We**'re**/They**'re helping**. ('re = are)	You/We/They **aren't helping**. (aren't = are not)
He**'s**/She**'s**/It**'s helping**. ('s = is)	He/She/It **isn't helping**. (isn't = is not)

Question	Short answer
Am I **helping**?	Yes, you **are**. No, you**'re not**.
Are you/we/they **helping**?	Yes, I **am**. / No, I**'m not**. Yes, we/they **are**. No, we/they **aren't**.
Is he/she/it **helping**?	Yes, he/she/it **is**. No, he/she/it **isn't**.

We form the present continuous with the present simple of the verb *to be* + the *-ing* form of the main verb.

When we add an adverb, it usually comes between *to be* and the main verb:

*A few pairs of these birds are **still** living in the wild.*

Spelling rules for present continuous

Verbs ending in *-e* change to *-ing*:
have → having

One-syllable verbs with a short vowel sound double the final consonant:
sit → sitting

Use

We use the present simple to talk about:
* a fact or permanent situation.
*Polar bears **have** thick fur.*
*They **live** in the Arctic.*

* something we do regularly.
*I **give** money to an environmental charity every month.*

We use the present continuous to talk about:
* something happening now, at this moment.
*This polar bear **is hunting** for seals.*

* events happening around now, during this period of time.
*Environmentalists **are trying** to save these endangered species.*

EXERCISES

1 Do you know the facts below? Complete the sentences with the correct form of these verbs.

become	carry	not drink
need	stay	taste

1 Crocodiles _____ their young to the water and leave them there.

2 Frogs _____ water.

3 A shark _____ to swim to stay alive.

4 Flamingos _____ pink because of the food they eat.

5 A butterfly _____ its food with its feet.

6 A panda cub _____ with its mother for about eighteen months.

2 Complete the text with the present continuous form of the verb.

My sister [1]_____ (study) Ecology and Wildlife Conservation at university. She and the other students on her course [2]_____ (learn) about the causes of environmental change and about possible solutions. Her university is in a small town between a large forest and the sea, so they [3]_____ (get) a great opportunity to study different habitats. This is her final year, so my sister [4]_____ (also write) an independent research project. Her research is on rainforests and she [5]_____ (hope) to work in Brazil after she graduates. She [6]_____ (not think) too much about that at the moment, however, because she has several exams to pass first!

LANGUAGE FOCUS Describing events in the present

We also use the present continuous to describe trends and changes.

*The situation **is becoming** more serious now.*

Note that there are some verbs that don't usually take a continuous form. These include *be, have*, verbs of feeling (*love, like, hate*) and verbs of thinking (*know, believe, understand*).

*I **hate** what is happening to the rainforest.*
*People **don't understand** how important it is to protect these animals.*

EXERCISES

1 Use the prompts and the present continuous form of the verbs to complete the conversation.

A: What / happen / in the Sahara? / climate change / make / it / hotter?
1 _____

B: Yes, it is. The temperatures / rise / every year.
2 _____

A: What is the effect of the hotter temperatures? it / get / drier?
3 _____

B: No / it / not / get drier. It / get / greener!
4 _____

A: So / more plants / grow / there / now?
5 _____

B: Yes, they are. People think the Sahara / slowly / become / like it was 12,000 years ago!
6 _____

2 Complete the phone conversation with the present simple or present continuous form of the verbs.

A: Hello. I ¹_____ to ask about the volunteering job at the zoo. (phone)

B: OK, great. What experience
²_____? (have)

A: I worked at an animal rescue centre in Uganda last year. And I
³_____ on my uncle's farm every summer. (work)

B: Great. So, ⁴_____ animals? (like)

A: Oh, yes, very much. I ⁵_____ primates, especially gorillas. But I
⁶_____ all animals. (love, like)

B: And what ⁷_____ at the moment? (do)

A: I ⁸_____ zoology at university. (study)

GRAMMAR Future plans

Form

Going to

Affirmative	Negative
I'm going to stay.	I'm not going to stay.
You're/We're/They're going to stay.	You/We/They aren't going to stay.
He's/She's/It's going to stay.	He/She/It isn't going to stay.

Question	Short answer
Am I going to stay?	Yes, you are. / No, you aren't.
Are you/we/they going to stay?	Yes, I am. / No, I'm not. Yes, we/they are. No, we/they aren't.
Is he/she/it going to stay?	Yes, he/she/it is. No, he/she/it isn't.

Present continuous for future

*I**'m seeing** my cousin on Saturday.*
*He **isn't coming** to the reunion.*

See Unit 1, page 137 for the full present continuous form.

Use

We use *going to* for:
• plans and intentions.
*I**'m going to** find out more about my father's family.*

We use the present continuous for:
• definite plans and arrangements.
*My brother**'s arriving** on Sunday.*

EXERCISES

1 Use these notes to make sentences about a couple's future travel plans. Use the *going to* form.

July

2nd	¹(John and me) Fly to New York
	²Stay with my brother and family for three nights
5th	³(me) Meet client – Mr Rose
	⁴(John) Visit MOMA and Empire State Building
6th	⁵(John) Travel to Washington DC for interview
	⁶(me) Train to Chicago to see cousin Judith
7th	⁷(John and me) Spend one night in hotel in NYC
8th	⁸(John and me) Return home

1 John and I *are going to fly to New York on 2nd July*.

2 We _____ .

3 I _____ .

4 John _____ .

5 He _____ .

6 I _____ .

7 We _____ .

8 We _____ .

2 Use the present continuous to make sentences about Lisa's plans and arrangements for the week.

Monday	Lunch with Nick
Tuesday	Meet Uncle Bernard
Wednesday	Ben arrives 4pm
Thursday	Mike and I visit Jo's new school
Friday	Mike, children and I go to school concert
Saturday	Take Simon swimming
Sunday	Mum and Dad come for dinner

1 On Monday *I'm having lunch with Nick* .

2 On Tuesday _____ .

3 On Wednesday _____ .

4 On Thursday _____ .

5 On Friday _____ .

6 On Saturday _____ .

7 On Sunday _____ .

LANGUAGE FOCUS Talking about future plans and arrangements

We can sometimes use either the present continuous or the *going to* form to describe the same future plan. We usually choose the present continuous when we consider the plan to be more certain and we have agreed it with other people.

*I **'m going to** see my family this weekend.* (I have a plan)
*I **'m seeing** my family this weekend.* (They are expecting me)

We normally use *going to* to talk about intentions in the more distant future.

*I **'m going to** visit my grandparents next summer.*

Note than when we use *going to* with the verb *to go*, we don't need to include *to go*. We tend to prefer the simpler form.

*When **are** you **going (to go)**?*
*I **'m going (to go)** in August.*

EXERCISES

1 Write questions to complete the conversation about arrangements for a family party. Use the present continuous.

A: [1]*Where is everybody meeting?*
B: Everybody is meeting at the hotel.

A: [2]_____
B: I'm arriving at 5pm to check everything is OK.

A: [3]_____
B: No, I'm not. I'm going on my own. Paolo is coming later.

A: [4]_____
B: Because he's picking up Sofia from the station. He can pick you up too if you want.

A: [5]_____
B: After dinner, Kristoff and I are both giving speeches.

A: [6]_____
B: No, you're not. The hotel is full. You're staying with us. Is that OK?

2 Use the prompts to make questions using *going to*. Then match the questions with the answers (a–f) to complete the conversation between two school friends.

1 When / you / get married?

_____

2 How many children / you / have?

_____

3 What / call them?

_____

4 Where / you / live?

_____

5 How / pay for your beautiful house?

_____

6 you / remember me when you're famous?

_____

a Sarah, Harriet, Jake and Lucian.

b I'm going to have a beautiful house in the countryside!

c When I'm 26.

d Of course. You're going to be my publisher!

e I'm going to be a famous writer and sell millions of books.

f I'm going to have two boys and two girls.

Grammar summary | UNIT 3

GRAMMAR Defining relative clauses

Form and use

The book **that** describes what happens before The Lord of the Rings *is called* The Hobbit.

The man **who** wrote She: A History of Adventure *also wrote another 55 novels.*

The place **where** the hobbits live in The Lord of the Rings *is called the Shire.*

To introduce relative clauses, we usually use:

- *who* for people.
  Draco Malfoy is a boy **who** hates Harry Potter.

- *that* for things.
  A Tale of Two Cities is a book **that** had a strong influence on me.

- *where* for places.
  Soldier Island is **where** the action happens in And Then There Were None.

We use defining relative clauses to give essential information about the thing (or person or place) we are talking about. Without this information the sentence would not make sense or communicate what we want to say.
  ~~Draco Malfoy is a boy hates Harry Potter.~~
  ~~Draco Malfoy is a boy.~~

In informal contexts we can also use *that* for people.
  The woman **that** came to speak at our school is quite a well-known writer.

We can also use *which* to talk about things. This is slightly more formal.
  The novel **which** I'd like to recommend is this year's Booker Prize winner.

Note that in informal contexts we can use *where* for events and situations (such as a party or concert), as well as books and films.
  Jaws is that film **where** a shark attacks people on a beach.
  It was the party **where** we met.

EXERCISES

1 Join the two sentences with the correct relative pronoun. Show all the possible relative pronouns.

  1 I'm reading a book. It's really good.
    I'm reading a book that/which is really good .

  2 It's about a young boy. He's a wizard.
    _____ .

  3 Hogwarts is a school. They train wizards there.
    _____ .

4 Harry has some friends. They are called Ron and Hermione.
  _____ .

5 Hedwig is an owl. He helps Harry.
  _____ .

6 There's a studio in London. You can see the Harry Potter sets.
  _____ .

2 Complete the descriptions with *who*, *that* or *where*. Use *who* wherever possible.

Anders Weberg is a Swedish artist [1]_____ is making a film [2]_____ is 720 hours long. He likes to make art [3]_____ people watch once – and then destroy it.

Waiting for Godot is a play by Samuel Beckett about two characters [4]_____ are waiting for something [5]_____ never happens and for someone [6]_____ never arrives. It was voted the most important play of the 20th century.

Bergen is the town in Norway [7]_____ a now-famous train journey started. In the first of many 'slow' TV programmes – including many [8]_____ were much longer – a seven-hour train journey between Bergen and Oslo became a seven-hour piece of film.

'Stairway to Heaven' is the song [9]_____ made the rock band Led Zeppelin famous. But the man [10]_____ wrote it, Robert Plant, hates it and never wants to play it again. He even gave money to a radio station [11]_____ promised never to play it.

EXTRA INFORMATION

Definitions with pronouns

We can use a pronoun to introduce the subject of the relative clause.
  It's **the book** that made her famous.
  They're **three children** who go on a journey of adventure.
  She's **the author** who sells more books than anyone else in the world.

Leaving out the relative pronoun

We can leave out *that* and *who* when they are the object of the sentence, but not when they are the subject.
  The actor **that** plays the main part is …
  The character (**that**) I like best is …

Grammar summary | UNIT 4

EXERCISES

1 Complete the descriptions using relative clauses. Start each one with the appropriate pronoun. Then match with the correct person, place or thing (a–f).

1 place / *The Hobbit* / is set

It's the place where The Hobbit _is set_ _____ .

2 man / wrote / best-selling French book *Le Petit Prince*

_____ .

3 word / means 'very scary'

_____ .

4 actress / played the White Witch in the Narnia films

_____ .

5 country / they filmed *The Lord of the Rings*

_____ .

6 most famous plays / Shakespeare wrote

_____ .

a *Hamlet* and *Romeo and Juliet*.
b Middle Earth
c Tilda Swinton
d Antoine de Saint-Exupéry
e New Zealand
f terrifying

2 Read the text and ~~cross out~~ the relative pronouns that you don't need.

As a child, I loved stories about poor or sad children ¹**who** have an experience ²**that** changes their lives completely. One story ³**that** I especially enjoyed was *The Secret Garden*. It's probably the book ⁴**that** I read most often during my childhood. It's about a girl ⁵**who** loses both her parents in India, so she goes to England to live in a big house ⁶**that** she finds lonely and boring. She becomes happier through the relationships ⁷**that** she makes with the people ⁸**who** she meets, and because of a secret garden ⁹**that** becomes her special place.

GRAMMAR Countable and uncountable nouns

Form and use

Countable nouns, e.g. *student* and *CD*, refer to things or people that can be counted. We can use them in the singular or plural. We can also use the indefinite article (*a/an*) or numbers before them.

> *A student* usually *spends* more money on entertainment than food.
> *I gave nearly 200 CDs to a charity shop yesterday.*

Uncountable nouns e.g. *research* and *music*, refer to things that can't be counted. We use uncountable nouns with a singular verb – they don't have a plural form. We don't use the indefinite article with uncountable nouns and we can't use them with numbers.

> *We're doing some new research on that.*
> (not *a research*)
> *The music is very loud in here!*

Note that with some uncountable words we can add *a piece of* in front of them to make them countable.

> *Our university did an interesting piece of research on music and happiness.*
> *The concert finished with a beautiful piece of music by Mozart.*

Some common uncountable nouns and their countable equivalent

Uncountable noun	Countable equivalent
travel	trip, journey
accommodation	place to live/stay
equipment	piece of equipment
vocabulary	word, expression
advice	piece of advice

Words we commonly use with countable and uncountable nouns

We use *much*, *many* and *a lot of* to talk about large quantities of something. We use *much* with uncountable nouns and *many* with countable nouns. We can use *a lot of* for both.

In positive sentences, we usually use *a lot of* or *lots of*, not *much* or *many*.

> *I can play a lot of songs on my guitar now.*

We use *a little* and *a few* to talk about small quantities. *A little* is used with uncountable nouns and *a few* with countable nouns.

> *I can play a little rock music.*
> *I know a few chords.*

We use *some* and *any* with countable and uncountable nouns. *Some* is usually used in positive sentences. *Any* is usually used in questions and negative sentences. However, we can use *some* in questions, suggestions or offers where we expect a positive answer.

> *I don't have **any** CDs now – it's all on my laptop.*
> *Excuse me, do you have **any** music by Megadeth?*
> *Do you want to listen to **some** music?*

EXERCISES

1 Choose the correct options to complete the text.

We went to see a musical last week. It was great, but there were ¹*a few / a little* things that we didn't like very much about it. Firstly, our seats cost ²*much / a lot of* money, but we couldn't see very well and there wasn't ³*much / some* room for our legs. And secondly, one of the actors had ⁴*any / some* problems remembering his words. However, it was a moving story and I loved the music. I didn't know ⁵*many / much* of the songs, but I would like to buy the soundtrack now.

2 Complete the sentences with these words.

any	a few	a lot of
many	much	some

1 How about watching _____ television to relax before we go out?

2 I wanted to see that play, but there weren't _____ tickets available, so, sadly, I couldn't.

3 There were _____ people trying to get into the festival, so I waited a long time.

4 I don't have _____ time, but I could meet you for an hour to have a look at the exhibition.

5 I don't know the words to _____ songs, but I do know _____ folk songs that my grandmother taught me.

LANGUAGE FOCUS Talking about quantity

Too much is used with uncountable nouns, and *too many* with countable nouns, to talk about having more of something than we need.

With *too much/many* and *how much/many* we can sometimes leave out the noun if it's clear what they refer to.

> *I drink **too much** coffee.*
> *I need to delete some photos. I have **too many**.*
> *Do you like country music? **How much** do you listen to?*
> ***How many** records do you have?*

Similarly, *some, any, a few* and *a little* can be used as pronouns if it is clear what they refer to.

> *Do you want some chocolate? Yes, just **a little**.*
> *Do you have **any** CDs? No, I don't have **any** now.*

Note that we say *a lot of* or *lots of* before a noun, but *a lot* or *lots* when we use them alone.

> *I had **a lot of** music on my phone, but I deleted it.*
> *Do you have many films? Yes, I have **lots** / **a lot**.*

EXERCISES

1 Complete the sentences with *too, too much, too many, how much* or *how many*.

1 I like working in a library as there is _____ noise at home.

2 My brother usually studies in a café – he can't work when it's _____ quiet!

3 I get hundreds of emails. I can't write back to them all. There are _____ !

4 _____ do you know about classical music?

5 If I work for _____ hours without a break, I start to make mistakes.

6 _____ hours a day do you spend sitting down?

2 ~~Cross out~~ the option that you CAN'T use.

1 Did they play *much / ~~many~~ / any* electronic music at the party?
Yes, they played *a little / a lot / much*.

2 I met *some / a few / any* interesting people in the music business.

3 I used to listen to *a lot of / lots of / lots* pop music, but now I don't really listen to *much / any / a little*.

4 How many people buy CDs these days?
Not *much / many / a lot*.

5 I speak *a little / a few / some* German. I signed up for an online course, but it goes *too / too much / a little* fast.

6 Do you go to *any / many / much* concerts?
Yes, *a few / a little / lots*. But they're expensive!

GRAMMAR Prepositions and adverbs of place

Form

Prepositions

*There's a unicorn **on the left of** the shield.*
*There are three ornamental flowers **on** the shield.*
*The mantle is **behind** the coat of arms.*

Adverbs

*There's a banner **at the top**.*

Above, below and *behind* can be used as prepositions or adverbs.

On the left/right of, at the top/bottom of, in front of and *on top of* are all prepositions. They can also be used as adverbs (without *of*).

*There's a motto **at the top of** the picture.* (preposition)
*The family name is **at the bottom**.* (adverb)

Use

We use prepositions of place to describe the location of things.

*There is a picture **on** the wall.*
*His coat is **in** the cupboard.*

Some prepositions change form to become adverbs (e.g. *in → inside*).

*His coat is **inside**.*

On, on top of and above

If something is *on* or *on top of* something, it is touching the thing it is placed on. *On top of* suggests it's in a higher position or covering the thing below it. We use *above* when something is in a higher position than something else but not touching it.

*There was a plate **on** the table.*
*They placed a flag **on top of** the mountain.*
*The soldier wore a coat **on top of** his uniform.*
*There was a painting **above** the bed.*

EXERCISES

1 Look at the photo. Complete the description using these words and phrases.

above	behind (x2)	below (x2)
in front of	on (x2)	on the left
on the right	on the right of	on top of

John Thomson was one of the first photographers to take pictures in China. This photo from 1868 shows a Chinese artist sitting [1]_____ the painting that he is working on. There is also another painting of a man – you can just see the head [2]_____ the one the artist is doing.

[3]_____ the artist's head there are two more paintings. The one [4]_____ is of a person sitting [5]_____ a chair and the one [6]_____ is a ship [7]_____ the sea. [8]_____ the ship there is another small picture.

[9]_____ the artist and [10]_____ the photo, there is a piece of furniture with a pot [11]_____ it. You can also see one more painting, or frame, [12]_____ his painting desk.

2 Decide if the sentences are correct (✓) or incorrect (✗). If incorrect, correct the mistake.

1 At top of the tower I can see a black bird.

2 There were two statues of dogs – one on the right and one on the left of the fireplace.

3 'Where is the mirror?' 'It's behind of the piano.'

4 The artist's name is at the bottom the painting.

5 In front of the house there was a very tall tree.

EXTRA INFORMATION

Other useful language for describing where things are in a picture

We use *in the foreground* to talk about what is nearest.

We use *in the background* to talk about what is furthest away.

We also use *in the top right / bottom left corner of the picture* and *in the middle of the picture*.

In front (of) and opposite

In front of is used when two things are both facing the same way (like seats in a theatre).

Opposite is used when two things or people are facing each other (as from two sides of a table).

> She smiled at the woman sitting **opposite** her.
> The wardrobe **in front of** the window blocked my view.

Through, across and over

Across and *over* can both mean on the other side of something, e.g. a river or a bridge. We use *over* for a wall or other high place. We use *through* for a tunnel, woods, etc.

> They travelled over a mountain, across a river and through a forest.

Note that we also use *through* to talk about crossing something out.

> The teacher put a big red line **through** my art history homework.

EXERCISES

1 Describe the painting using phrases with *foreground*, *background*, *middle* and *corner*.

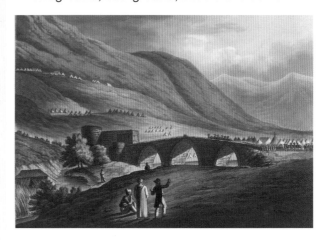

1 _____ there are three people.
2 _____ there is a large bridge.
3 _____ there is a patch of clear sky.
4 _____ there are some large mountains.
5 _____ there is a bush and a low building.

2 Look at the painting again and choose the correct options.

1 If you look closely you can see that there are lots of people and animals walking *through / across* the bridge.

2 There is a man standing on the river bank *opposite / in front of* the low building.

3 On the left there are two large trees *in front of / opposite* a tower.

4 If you look *through / over* the bridge you can see two tents on the other side of the river.

5 There are some tents high up on the mountain side and there are some more *on / at* the bottom of the mountain.

6 I think it would be very difficult to get *through / over* those mountains.

GRAMMAR Reported speech

Form

Direct speech	Reported speech
Sara: I **like** reggae music.	Sara said that she **liked** reggae music.
Jaime: I **don't** understand abstract art.	Jaime said he **didn't** understand abstract art.
May: I **will** be at the arts centre at 5pm.	May said she **would** be at the arts centre at 5pm.
Leo: I **can't** play an instrument.	Leo said he **couldn't** play an instrument.

When we report what someone says, the verb moves one tense back (e.g. from present simple to past simple). We do this even if what someone said then is still true.

'I live near a wonderful art gallery.'

→ She said (that) she lived near a wonderful art gallery. (She still lives there)

Note that we often add *that* before the words we report. However, it is not usually necessary.

Would, could, should

These words do not change when we report them.

*'I **could** learn a lot from him.'*

*→ She said she **could** learn a lot from him.*

Pronoun, adjective and adverb changes

If the speaker changes, or we are talking about what someone said at a different time, we may also need to change other words in the sentence.

I → he/she	this → the or that
we → they	tomorrow → the next day
my → his/her	here → there

*'I like **this** idea.'*

*→ **She** said she liked **the/that** idea.*

(we use *the* if it's not clear what the idea is)

*I said, '**I** often paint **my** own face.'*

*→ I said that **I** often painted **my** own face.*

(same speaker, different time)

*He said, '**I** often paint **my** own face.'*

*→ He said **he** often painted **his** own face.*

(different speaker, different time)

Use

We use reported speech to describe what someone says when we don't need or want to use their exact words. We often use reported speech to summarize a conversation, meeting or a talk.

EXERCISES

1 Complete these reported sentences.

1 'I find Frida Kahlo very inspiring', he said.
He said that _____ Frida Kahlo very inspiring.

2 'We study Anne Frank at school', she said.
She said _____ Anne Frank at school.

3 'Bob Marley's music still sounds fresh', the journalist said.
The journalist said that _____ fresh.

4 Coco Chanel said, 'A girl should be two things: classy and fabulous.'
Coco Chanel said that _____: classy and fabulous.

5 Marta: 'I want to live more simply, like Mahatma Gandhi.'
Marta said _____ more simply, like Mahatma Gandhi.

6 Stephen Hawking said recently, 'I am more convinced than ever that we are not alone.'
Stephen Hawking said recently _____ than ever that we were not alone.

2 Report these statements. Think about any additional words that need to change in the reported version.

1 Safi and Adam: 'We want to improve people's lives – there are many problems here.'
_____ .

2 Liban: 'I try to treat people in the way I want people to treat me.'
_____ .

3 The company Inspiraquote said, 'People come to our quotes website to get inspiration.'
_____ .

4 Tom said, 'I'd like to buy this book about Mandela.'
_____ .

LANGUAGE FOCUS Reporting what people say

We use *say* when there is no object after the verb (when we don't say who we are talking to). We use *tell* when there is an object (when we mention who we are speaking to).

> I **said** it was interesting.
> I **told him** it was interesting.

We use *tell* + object + *to* + infinitive when we are reporting orders, instructions or advice.

> 'Remember Gandhi's message.'
> → He **told me to remember** Gandhi's message.

If the instruction is negative, we add *not*.

> '**Don't** forget my words.'
> → He told me **not** to forget his words.

EXERCISES

1 Read a grandmother's advice to her grandson. Report the advice using *tell*.

1 Work hard and be honest.
   My grandmother told me to work hard and be honest.

2 Decide who you want to be.
   She _____ .

3 Don't try to change other people.
   _____ .

4 Respect the older generation.
   _____ .

5 Don't forget to say sorry when you do something wrong.
   _____ .

6 It's more important to be kind than to be right.
   _____ .

2 Choose the correct options to complete the sentences.

1 Bob Marley *said / told* that we needed to free our own minds.

2 Marley's song tells us *that we loved / to love* the life we live and lead the life we love.

3 He *told / said* an interviewer in 1992 that he didn't have education, he had inspiration.

4 Bob Marley didn't think that possessions made people rich. He *said / told* to people that life was his richness.

5 In 'Three little birds', he tells us *we don't worry / not to worry* about a thing.

6 Bob Marley said that people who lived for others *will / would* live again.

GRAMMAR *will* for predictions

Form and use

We use *will* + infinitive (without *to*) to talk about things we imagine happening in the future (or know or believe will happen).

> I think more people **will** grow their own vegetables.
> The world **will** need 30 per cent more food.

We usually contract *will* with pronouns.

> **It'll** be harder to feed everyone.

We usually contract the negative (*will not*) to *won't*.

> We **won't** eat so much wild fish in the future.

We often use predictions with verbs of opinion and emotion, for example, *believe, think, imagine, fear, hope, be sure, expect*.

> I **believe** there will be less meat available.

EXERCISES

1 Complete the sentences. Use contractions where possible.

1 I think people _____ (produce) meat in a way that is less cruel to animals.

2 Farmers fear that bad weather _____ (destroy) a lot of their land.

3 I'm worried we _____ (not / change) quickly enough.

4 Scientists argue that higher temperatures _____ (change) the food we grow.

5 I hope people _____ (not / be) so wasteful with resources.

6 I'm sure I _____ (see) changes I can't imagine yet.

2 Look at someone's plans and predictions. Write sentences using *going to* and *will*.

My plans	Predictions for my future life
[1]Move to countryside	[2]Meet some nice new people in the village (I imagine)
[3]Not work so much	[4]Have no grandchildren for many years (I fear)
[5]Learn to grow my own vegetables	[6]Stay healthy (I hope)

1 *I'm going to move to the countryside* .
2 _____ .
3 _____ .
4 _____ .
5 _____ .
6 _____ .

LANGUAGE FOCUS Discussing the future

We can show how certain we are about a prediction by using adverbs such as *definitely* and *probably*. Note that *probably* and *definitely* usually go between *will* and the main verb.

> Scientists **will probably develop** different foods.
> They **will definitely need** to feed more people.

In a negative prediction, the adverb goes before *won't*.

> We **definitely won't eat** so much protein.

Questions with *will* have no auxiliary *do*.

> **Will** people eat more food that is locally produced?
> Yes, they **will**. / No, they **won't**.

We can also ask *wh-* questions about the future.

> **How will** eating habits change?
> **When will** people start to adapt?

EXERCISES

1 Write questions for the predictions.

1 A: *What will people eat* ?
B: People will probably eat more insects.

2 A: Where _____ ?
B: People will live in more energy-efficient houses.

3 A: _____ ?
B: No, it won't. I think food will be more expensive.

4 A: _____ ?
B: I hope we'll travel on bikes more.

5 A: _____ ?
B: I don't know. I think some people will be healthier and others won't.

6 A: _____ ?
B: Yes, I think many people will live longer.

2 Put the adverbs in the correct place in the sentences.

1 We will find cures for some diseases. (definitely)

2 People will live on other planets. (probably)

3 Robots won't organize our lives. (probably)

4 Driverless cars will be normal. (probably)

5 Phones won't look like they do now. (definitely)

6 There will be technology that we can't predict! (definitely)

GRAMMAR Phrasal verbs

Form

Phrasal verbs are verbs that combine a verb with a particle (or preposition) to create a new verb. The new verb often has a different meaning from the two parts used separately. For example, we can't guess the meaning of this sentence by knowing the meaning of *take* and *up*.

> I **took up** Danish. (= I started to learn Danish)

Common particles or prepositions include *about*, *across*, *away*, *back*, *down*, *in*, *off*, *out*, *up*, etc.

Phrasal verbs usually have two parts (*clean up*, *check out*, etc.), but can also have three parts (*hang out with*, *meet up with*, *look forward to*).

There are two main kinds of phrasal verbs: separable and inseparable. With inseparable verbs (*look at*, *go out*) we can't separate the verb from the particle.

> I **looked at** a new flat today. (~~I looked a new flat at today~~)

With separable verbs (*put on*, *take off*) we can separate the verb and the particle with a noun or a pronoun. Note that the pronoun can ONLY go between the verb and the particle.

> I **put on** my coat as I left.
> I **put** my coat **on** as I left.
> I **took** it **off** when I got there. (~~I took off it~~)

Use

Phrasal verbs are often quite informal and idiomatic. We can sometimes replace a phrasal verb with a single verb that has a similar, but more formal, meaning. For example, *come back = return*, *come in = enter*, *look for = search*. However, you will sound more natural if you can learn and use some of the more common phrasal verbs.

EXERCISES

1 Replace the words in bold with the correct form of the phrasal verb in brackets.

1 We **had meals in restaurants** nearly every night when we were in Cadiz. (eat out)

_____

2 We are **leaving our house** in a month. We decided we wanted to live abroad. (move out)

_____

3 There was lots to explore in Helsinki so we **left the hotel** quite early. (set off)

_____

4 We found a beautiful shop in Milan and **dressed ourselves in** lots of different clothes. (try on)

_____

5 Our neighbours **gave food and water to** our cat while we were in Hamburg for the weekend. (look after)

_____

6 I've got an old school friend in Lyon who I'm going to **see and chat to** while I'm there. (meet up with)

_____

2 Rewrite the sentences. Replace the noun with the correct pronoun.

1 I phoned up my Hungarian friend.
_I phoned him/her up_____ .

2 My mother took up Italian last year.
My _____ .

3 Luckily, I didn't throw away the old guide books.

_____ .

4 I finally figured out the transport system.

_____ .

5 We looked up the train times.

_____ .

6 I showed George around my university.

_____ .

EXTRA INFORMATION

Note that some phrasal verbs are transitive (take an object) e.g. _look at,_ and some are intransitive (don't take an object) e.g. _eat out._

We're **looking at** a new house on Saturday.
We enjoyed Cadiz as it was a great place to **eat out**.

Some verbs can be transitive or intransitive depending on the context.
You don't need a car to **get around** the city.
My grandmother finds it difficult to **get around**.

Intransitive verbs are always inseparable, but transitive verbs can be separable or inseparable.
I **grew up** in a small town. (inseparable, intransitive)
Let's **check out** the shops near here. (separable, transitive)
I'm **looking for** a new flat in a cheaper area. (inseparable, transitive)

EXERCISES

1 Complete the phrasal verbs with _look_. Use these particles and prepositions. Which three sentences have intransitive verbs?

after	around (x2)	back	for
forward	out	up	

1 When I look _____, I have such happy memories of our holiday in Kenya.

2 I looked _____ the word for 'return ticket' online.

3 I found a dog that didn't have an owner so I looked _____ it.

4 I look _____ a mixture of peace and liveliness in a city.

5 I had some time to spare so I looked _____ the old town.

6 Look _____! There's a car coming.

7 I'm really looking _____ to our weekend away.

8 Please come in and look _____. You don't need to buy anything.

2 Find and correct three mistakes in the conversation.

A: I can't wait for the weekend.
B: Yes, I'm really looking forward it to.
A: Do you want to check out the new _Star Wars_ film?
B: Good idea. We can meet up with Dave, too.
A: Yeah, it's a while since I hung out him.
B: OK, I'll probably drive, so I can pick up you.

GRAMMAR *will* for offers and first conditionals

Form and use

First conditional

*If they **come**, we**'ll have** enough people.*
*If they **don't come**, we **won't have** enough people.*

if clause	main clause
if + present simple	will + infinitive without to

We use the first conditional to show that if one thing happens (possible future action), another will also happen (result of the possible future action).

*If we **raise** enough money, we **will buy** some new equipment for the children's centre.*

Offers

We form offers by using *will* + infinitive without *to*. This shows we are happy to do something.

*I**'ll do** it!*
*Roy and I **will** make the food.*
A: *Can somebody help me lift this?*
B: *I **will**.*

EXERCISES

1 Match the two parts to make sentences.

  1 If we call people to ask them for money,

  2 If you use social media,

  3 If we send letters,

  4 If I knock on people's doors,

  5 If we host an event,

  a some people will give money, but others will be annoyed that I'm there.

  b it'll be a lot of work, but people will have fun and we'll raise lots of money.

  c they'll put the phone down.

  d people will forget to donate because they see so much stuff on the Internet.

  e they'll end up in the paper recycling bin!

2 You are helping with a charity event. Make offers by combining a verb from box A with a word or phrase from box B. Use each option once. Then list the offers in a logical order. There may be more than one possible order.

A

book	clean up	contact
~~make~~	organize	print

B

afterwards	the food	some sponsors
~~a list of people to invite~~		the venue
some tickets		

1 *I'll make a list of people to invite*   .
2 _____ .
3 _____ .
4 _____ .
5 _____ .
6 _____ .

LANGUAGE FOCUS Making offers and describing possible future events

To make negative conditional sentences we use *don't* in the *if* clause and *will not* (*won't*) in the main clause.

*If we **don't** all help, we **won't** finish until late.*

We can change the order of the conditional. Note that we only use a comma when the *if* clause comes first.

*If we all **help**, we**'ll finish** earlier.*
*We**'ll finish** earlier **if** we all **help**.*

We can also make conditional questions.

*If I **help** on Friday, **will** you **help** on Saturday?*
***Will** you **help** on Friday **if** I **help** on Saturday?*

We can combine an offer with a conditional.

*If I **have** time on Saturday, I**'ll take** your old clothes to the charity shop.*
*I**'ll take** your old clothes to the charity shop **if** I **have** time on Saturday.*

EXERCISES

1 Choose the correct options to complete the conversations.

A: Will you ¹*helping / help* make some cakes for the fundraiser?

B: Yes, of course I ²*will / won't*. I'll ³*to make / make* some tonight.

A: If I ⁴*will call / call* the sponsors, ⁵*will you / you will* contact the venue?

B: Yes, sure. ⁶*I do / I'll do* it now if you ⁷*have / will have* the phone number.

A: If we ⁸*don't / won't* start raising money now, people ⁹*won't / don't* have enough to eat over the winter.

B: I agree. If I ¹⁰*get / got* the collection boxes tonight, ¹¹*you / will you* organize a door-to-door collection at the weekend?

A: Yes, ¹²*I will / I'll*.

2 Put the words and phrases in the correct order to make conditional sentences and questions. Add commas where they are needed.

1 invite / We'll / if / a few famous people / good publicity / we / get

_____

2 to raise awareness / set up / We'll / help / a website / if / we

_____

3 will / find / people / can pay / If / they / it easier / online

_____

4 use / Will / come / if / don't / enough people / social media / we / ?

_____

5 don't / They / donate / if / explain / won't / we / what the charity does

_____

6 If / my car / bring / you / need / to drive / I'll

_____

7 Will / raise / on a Saturday / more money / we / if / we hold / the event / ?

_____

8 If / them / design / you / print / the tickets / will / I / ?

_____

GRAMMAR Adverbs and adverbial phrases

Form and use

Adverbials of time

These usually go at the end of the sentence or clause. These tell us *when* something happens.
   *Tom plays brain games on his phone **every day**.*

We can use simple adverbs such as *now* and *then*, but we often use adverbial phrases like *next week*, *early one morning*, *in a few days*, etc. If we put adverbials of time at the start of the sentence, it puts more emphasis on the time. This position is also more used in written language.
   *Your brain stops growing **at the age of 25**.*
   ***At the age of 25**, your brain stops growing.*

Adverbs of manner

These adverbs usually go at the end of the sentence. They tell us *how* something happens.
   *She's studying **quietly**.*

Adverbs of manner sometimes go in the middle of the sentence (before the main verb or between the auxiliary and main verb) if the adverb is not the main focus of the message.
   *She **quickly** finished the test.* (focus on finishing)
   *She finished the test **quickly**.* (focus on how fast)

Adverbs of attitude

These go at the start of the sentence and are followed by a comma. They express the speaker's attitude towards an action. They usually refer to the content of the whole sentence rather than just the verb.
   ***Interestingly**, your brain can't feel pain.*

EXERCISES

1 Put the adverb in the best place in the sentence. Add a comma where needed.

1 A baby's brain is almost the same size as an adult's. (apparently)

_____ .

2 If we read we retain more information. (slowly)

_____ .

3 We have to write dreams down if we want to remember them. (immediately)

_____ .

4 Studies show that people who eat seafood have lower rates of dementia. (once a week)

_____ .

5 Reading aloud and talking to a child promotes brain development. (not surprisingly)

_____ .

2 ~~Cross out~~ the option you CAN'T use in each sentence.

1 *During / At / In* the summer term, we learned about memory.

2 *After / Following / Next* the operation, he had no sensation in his hands.

3 He won a competition *last month / for a month / a month ago*.

4 I have to finish my project *in a day or two / in a couple of days / in both days*.

5 *When / As / When I was* a child, I started having strange dreams.

6 Does the new course start *on / next / in* Tuesday?

7 I have my exams *the week after next / a fortnight / in a couple of weeks*.

8 *After a few hours, / After a while, / After,* he couldn't concentrate any more.

EXTRA INFORMATION

Irregular forms

There are some adjectives and adverbs that have the same form, such as *fast* and *hard*. Some adverbs have two forms, such as *free* (without payment) and *freely* (without limits or restrictions).

Spelling rules

Adjectives ending in *-y* usually change to *-ily* in the adverb.

pret**ty** → prett**ily**, hap**py** → happ**ily**

The following are all both adverbs and adjectives: *daily, monthly, weekly, yearly* and *early*.

*It's important to exercise **weekly**.*
***Weekly** exercise is important.*

Two meanings

The same adverb can sometimes be used as an adverb of manner or of attitude, depending how and where it is used in the sentence.

***Naturally**, he did better than all his classmates in the exam.* (of course he did)
*He explained the problem very **naturally**.* (in a very natural manner)

EXERCISES

1 Complete the sentences with these adverbs.

daily	fast	hard	late	well

1 If you work _____ and concentrate, you could get a very good result.

2 I was worried about handing my essay in _____.

3 I didn't want to do the puzzle too _____ in case I made a mistake.

4 I meditate _____ to help my concentration.

5 Doing more exercise can help the brain work _____.

2 Make adverbs from the adjectives in brackets. Put them in the correct place in these pairs of sentences.

1 (happy)

a Pat spent the whole day doing brain games.

_____

b He didn't find the brain games difficult.

_____

2 (clear)

a After a whole day of studying I couldn't see!

_____

b I need to take more breaks when I'm studying.

_____

3 (free)

a There are some interesting lectures which you can access online.

_____

b Research shows that there is most activity in the brain when our thoughts wander.

_____

GRAMMAR Present perfect

Form

Affirmative	Negative
I/You/We/They **have** slept.	I/You/We/They **haven't slept**. (haven't = have not)
He/She/It **has** slept.	He/She/It **hasn't slept**. (hasn't = has not)

Question	Short answer
Have I/you/we/they slept?	Yes, you/I/we/they **have**. No, you/I/we/they **haven't**.
Has he/she/it slept?	Yes, he/she/it **has**. No, he/she/it **hasn't**.

The present perfect is formed with the auxiliary verb *have* + the past participle of the verb. The past participle of a regular verb is formed in the same way as the past simple, i.e. infinitive + -ed.
> work → work**ed**

Spelling rules

There are also many irregular past participles. See the verb list on page 174.

Note that the verb *go* has two forms in the present perfect: *been* and *gone*. *Been* describes going somewhere and coming back. *Gone* describes going somewhere and still being there.
> She's **gone** camping. (She is away camping now)
> She's **been** camping. (She is not camping now – we are talking about her past experience)

Use

We use the present perfect to describe an event that happened sometime in the past, but we don't know exactly when.
> Liz **has swum** in a lake.

We use the past simple to describe an event that happened at a definite time in the past.
> Liz **swam** across Lake Windermere last year.

When we provide more details about an experience, we usually use the past simple.
> I**'ve been** skiing twice. I **went** once with my family and another time with my class.

Sometimes the time reference can be implied.
> I**'ve climbed** a mountain. It **was** very tiring. (We don't say when, but we are referring to a specific event)

EXERCISES

1 Complete the experiences with the present perfect form of the verb. Use contractions where possible.

1 We _____ (eat) wild strawberries.
2 My children _____ (not collect) eggs from a chicken.
3 He _____ (go) to a bird centre.
4 We _____ (never grow) our own vegetables.
5 Tim _____ (sleep) on a beach.
6 He _____ (not study) much about nature at school yet.

2 Complete the follow-up sentences with the past simple form of the verbs. Then match them with the experiences from Exercise 1.

a But a friend _____ me some tomato plants, so I _____ them on Saturday. (give, plant)
b Last term, he _____ about history and _____ about other cultures. (learn, read)
c They _____ really sweet. We _____ them! (be, love)
d He _____ a book so he _____ identify them. (buy, can)
e But they _____ the goats and chickens when we _____ to a farm. (feed, go)
f He _____ much rest though because the police _____ to tell him it wasn't allowed. (not get, come)

LANGUAGE FOCUS Talking about past experiences

Note that we often use *ever* in questions about experience to add emphasis. Similarly, we often use *never* in a negative response.
> A: *Have you **ever** been skiing?*
> B: *No, **never**. / No, I've **never** been skiing.*

Comparing experiences

Me too or *so have I* are two ways of saying we've had the same experience as someone.
> A: *I**'ve picked** wild mushrooms.*
> B: *Me too. / So have I.*

Me neither or *neither have I* are used when we are talking about experiences we haven't had.
> A: *I**'ve never seen** a bear.*
> B: *Me neither. / Neither have I.*

Note that we only use the *me too* and *me neither* forms in the first person. For second and third persons we use *so have they, neither has he*, etc.

EXERCISES

1 Make present perfect questions and short answers. If you don't know the past participle of the verb, use the list on page 174.

1 A: you / ever / see / elephants in the wild / ?

_____

B: Yes, _____.

2 A: you / ever / find / eggs in a bird's nest / ?

_____

B: No, _____.

3 A: your sister / ever / ride / a horse / ?

_____

B: Yes, _____.

4 A: you and your family / ever / keep chickens / ?

_____

B: No, _____.

5 A: any of your friends / ever / hear / an owl / ?

_____

B: Yes, _____.

6 A: he / ever / run on a beach with no shoes on / ?

_____

B: Yes, _____.

2 Complete the statements with these words. Then respond to the statements.

been	caught	had
~~held~~	seen	taught

1 I've ___*held*___ a snake.
(same): ___*So have I*___ .

2 I've never _____ in the woods at night.
(same): _____ .

3 I've _____ my children not to be scared of spiders.
(different): _____ .

4 We've never _____ a dog or a cat.
(same): _____ .

5 I've never _____ a butterfly in our garden.
(different): _____ .

6 I've _____ a fish in the sea.
(same): _____ .

GRAMMAR The passive

Form and use

	Active	Passive
Present	They **display** a lot of old coins at the museum.	A lot of old coins **are displayed** at the museum.
Past	People **found** many of the coins in Greece.	Many of the coins **were found** in Greece.

We make the passive form with _to be_ + the past participle of the verb used in the active sentence.
People **know** Tutankhamun as the Boy King.
Tutankhamun **is known** as the Boy King.

We usually prefer to use the passive:

• when we don't want to say who performs the action, or we don't know who it is.
The castle **was burned** to the ground.

• where the action (what happens) is more important than the 'doer' (who performs the action).
Roman coins **are found** throughout Europe.

If we want to know who performed the verb in a passive sentence, we can add a phrase with _by_. The subject of the active sentence becomes the 'agent' of the passive sentence.
**Howard Carter** discovered Tutankhamun in 1922.
Tutankhamun was discovered in 1922 **by Howard Carter**.

We only use _by_ + agent where it adds information. In many cases we don't need to mention the agent at all.
The bones **were put** on display.

The passive is often used in news reports, and in scientific and academic contexts.
The ruins of Pompeii **were buried** under volcanic ash for 1,700 years.
They **are visited** by around three million people a year.

The present passive is also often used to describe processes, for example, to show how something is made or done.
First, an archaeologist **is contacted** ...

EXERCISES

1 Rewrite each sentence using the past form of the passive. Use *by* only where it adds information to the sentence.

1 The Oscans built Pompeii in the 6th or 7th century BC.

Pompeii was built by the Oscans in the 6th or 7th century BC.

2 The Romans took the city over in the 4th century BC.

_____ .

3 After the volcano, people lost Pompeii for over 1,500 years.

_____ .

4 Someone first discovered the lost city in 1599.

_____ .

5 Then, Rocque Joaquín de Alcubierre rediscovered it in 1748.

_____ .

2 Complete this text about the processes involved in an archaeological dig. Use the present passive.

First of all, a site [1]_____ (chose). The ground [2]_____ (divide) into squares with rope and string. This is so that the archaeologists know exactly where something [3]_____ (find). Holes [4]_____ (dig) in the ground by the archaeologists, and all the objects they find [5]_____ (put) into small bags. These [6]_____ (carefully / label). A lot of care [7]_____ (take) so that the objects [8]_____ (not / break).

LANGUAGE FOCUS Talking about discoveries

We can make questions using the passive.

Is the statue **covered** in gold?
Yes, it **is**. / No it **isn't**.

Were the weapons **made** of iron?
Yes, they **were**. / No, they **weren't**.

Where were the weapons made?
Who were they **made by**?

EXERCISES

1 Make passive questions about the information in bold in the text. Use the prompts below.

In 1942, [1]**some 4th century Roman 'treasure'** was found in Mildenhall, Suffolk, in the east of the UK. All the bowls and spoons were made of [2]**silver**. This treasure was discovered [3]**by a farmer**, who didn't at first realize what it was. [4]**In 1946**, it was acquired by the British Museum. It was of such high quality that experts weren't sure if these things were really Roman. But we now know that they were, because lots more Roman treasure (the 'Hoxne hoard') was found [5]**50 years later**, in the same part of the country. This hoard is displayed [6]**in the British Museum** and the treasure is now seen by [7]**thousands of visitors** every year.

1 What / find / 1942 / ?
What was found in 1942?

2 What / bowls and spoons / made of / ?
_____

3 Who / discover / treasure / ?
_____

4 When / British Museum / acquire / it / ?
_____

5 When / find / Hoxne hoard / ?
_____

6 Where / display / Hoxne hoard / ?
_____

7 Who / see / the treasure / ?
_____

2 Correct the mistake in each sentence.

1 The archaeologist has invited to give a talk about his discoveries.

2 Before they are displaying in a museum, all the objects are cleaned.

3 Mosasaurus dinosaur bones were dig up in 1764.

4 The cave paintings in El Castillo was discovered by Hermilio Alcalde del Río.

5 The Rosetta Stone was originally displayed without protection, but in 1847 it put in a special case.

6 Lots of Roman treasure was showed for the first time in 2016 at the Museum of Liverpool.

Communication activities

Unit 1.2 Exercise 10, page 13

STUDENT A

1 Look at this information about the Bengal tiger. Ask Student B questions to complete the information.

Bengal tiger

Where do Bengal tigers live?

They live in …

Who are local police arresting?

They are arresting …

- **Population** 2,800
- **Where they live** _____
- **Conservation status** _____
- **Reason** _____

How people are helping
- Local police are arresting _____ .
- Tour companies are offering _____ .
- Park rangers are receiving additional training _____ .

2 Answer Student B's questions about the kiwi.

Kiwi

- **Population** 50,000–60,000
- **Where they live** New Zealand
- **Conservation status** threatened
- **Reason** habitat loss and predators such as cats and rats

How people are helping
- Scientists are increasing bird numbers through breeding programmes.
- People are building fences to keep predators away.
- Volunteers are removing eggs from the wild and then returning the birds to the wild.

Unit 1.5 Exercise 2, page 18

STUDENT A

Indian python
Status
near threatened
Why are numbers declining?
hunting, human conflict
Why do they need saving?
• They help control pests such as rats and rabbits.
• They help keep diseases from rats spreading.
Something to consider
It is extremely rare for an Indian python to attack a human.

Unit 2.5 Exercise 1, page 28

STUDENT A

Alice is Steve's wife.
Pam is Steve's daughter.
Rex is Cindy's husband.
Susan is Cindy's daughter.
Max is Maggie's husband.
Cindy is Maggie's mother-in-law.
Cindy is John's daughter.
Max is John's grandson.

Unit 1.2 Exercise 10, page 13

STUDENT B

1 Answer Student A's questions about the Bengal tiger.

Bengal tiger

- **Population** 2,800
- **Where they live** India, Nepal, Bangladesh
- **Conservation status** endangered
- **Reason** poaching and habitat loss

How people are helping

- Local police are arresting more poachers.
- Tour companies are offering trips to see them in the wild.
- Park rangers are receiving additional training.

2 Look at this information about the kiwi. Ask Student A questions to complete the information.

> Where do kiwis live?

> They live in …

> How are scientists increasing bird numbers?

> They're increasing bird numbers through …

Kiwi

- **Population** 50,000–60,000
- **Where they live** _____
- **Conservation status** _____
- **Reason** _____

How people are helping

- Scientists are increasing bird numbers through _____ .
- People are building _____ to keep predators away.
- Volunteers are removing eggs from the wild and then returning the birds to the wild.

Unit 1.5 Exercise 2, page 18

STUDENT B

Frégate Island beetle

Status
critically endangered

Why are numbers declining?
natural disasters, habitat loss

Why do they need saving?

- They are unique because they only live on one two-square-kilometre island.
- They are critically endangered and could become extinct very soon without help.

Something to consider
Humans have only recently started living on their island in the Indian Ocean.

Unit 2.5 Exercise 1, page 28

STUDENT B

Rex is Alice's son.

Susan is Alice's granddaughter.

Cindy is Mike's sister.

Rex is Mike's brother-in-law.

Jessica is Steve's sister.

Alice is Jessica's sister-in-law.

John is Becky's husband.

Susan is Becky's granddaughter.

Unit 9.5 Exercise 1, page 102

CHARITY APPEALS		
Books for Good is seeking donations. If you donate £5, we will provide ten textbooks to local schoolchildren in need. If you donate £10, we will send twenty textbooks and a dictionary. Please help!	After the recent storm that hit a South Pacific island, **Tsunami Relief** is asking for cash donations to help clothe and feed residents. Donate whatever you can – £20, £40, or more.	Help **Trees Trees Trees** replant City Park after the recent fire. If you donate £20, we will plant a tree in your name. We are also looking for volunteers to help with the planting.
The **City Square Homeless Centre** is asking for donations to help buy food for the homeless. We will be at City Square this weekend collecting donations. See you there!	People in deserts around the world need more fresh water. If you donate £60, a village will use the money to buy local materials to build a well. Contact the charity **Well Wishers** to make a direct donation to a village.	The Panamanian Golden Frog is nearly extinct because of disease. **Frog Friends** is asking for donations to fund research and find ways to reintroduce the frogs into the wild.

Unit 12.2 Exercise 9, page 129

STUDENT A

Read each question and the three choices to your partner. Mark your partner's guesses. Then see how many questions your partner got correct. (Correct answers are in **bold**.)

1 Easter Island is famous for its large statues. Where is Easter Island?

   a the Indian Ocean   b the Atlantic Ocean   c **the Pacific Ocean**

2 When were the pyramids of Egypt built?

   a 6000 BC   b **2700 BC**   c 100 AD

3 Where is Machu Picchu located?

   a **Peru**   b Egypt   c Italy

4 What volcano was Pompeii built next to?

   a **Vesuvius**   b Etna   c Krakatoa

5 Where were the earliest human fossils found?

   a in Europe   b **in Africa**   c in Asia

Unit 10.2 Exercise 9, page 109

Try the logic puzzle with a partner. Read the sentences and complete the results table.

1 John finished ahead of the English swimmer.

2 Roger swam well and won the race easily.

3 Surprisingly, Paul, aged 37, finished ahead of the eighteen-year-old swimmer.

4 Mark was the youngest swimmer.

5 The Australian swimmer was 32 years old.

6 There was one swimmer from New Zealand.

7 A 27-year-old finished in third place.

8 The South African swimmer was younger than Paul.

Men's 100m Freestyle – Final Standings

Position	Name	Age	Country
1			
2			
3			
4			

Unit 1.5 Exercise 2, page 18

STUDENT C

Bluefin tuna

Status
endangered
Why are numbers declining?
popularity as food, overfishing
Why do they need saving?
• Bluefin tuna are predators. They keep smaller fish numbers in check.
• Sharks feed on bluefin tuna. Fewer tuna would mean fewer sharks.
Something to consider
It's illegal to hunt bluefin tuna in many places, but many people still do.

Unit 2.5 Exercise 1, page 28

STUDENT C

Rex is Pam's brother.
Cindy is Pam's sister-in-law.
Max is Susan's brother.
Pam is Susan's aunt.
Steve is Tom's son.
Rex is Tom's grandson.
Becky is Ed's daughter.
Susan is Ed's great-granddaughter.

Unit 10.1 Exercise 10, page 107

Try the brain games below with a partner. Do you find them easy or difficult?

1 Count each *f* in this sentence.

Fifty-five fireflies flew from the top to the bottom of the fig tree.

2 How many squares can you see?

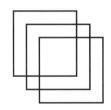

Unit 12.2 Exercise 9, page 129

STUDENT B

Read each question and the three choices to your partner. Mark your partner's guesses.
Then see how many questions your partner got correct. (Correct answers are in **bold**.)

1 When did Christopher Columbus first visit the Americas?
   a **1492**   b 1522   c 1576

2 When was the wreck of *Titanic* found?
   a **1985**   b 1997   c 2005

3 When was the dwarf planet Pluto discovered?
   a 1850   b **1930**   c 1990

4 What was painted on the walls of the Altamira cave?
   a writing   b a map   c **hunters and animals**

5 Besides hieroglyphics, what other language was included on the Rosetta Stone?
   a English   b **Greek**   c French

Unit 12.5 Exercise 1, page 134

STUDENT A

Look at the photo below. You and your team of archaeologists recently found this artefact in the ground.
Student B is going to interview you about your discovery. Use your imagination and prepare notes to
answer any questions. Use the prompts below to help.

What exactly is it?

When / Where was it discovered?

How old is it?

Why is it important?

Unit 12.5 Exercise 2, page 134

STUDENT B

Look at the photo below. You and your team of archaeologists recently found this artefact in the ground. Student A is going to interview you about your discovery. Use your imagination and prepare notes to answer any questions. Use the prompts below to help.

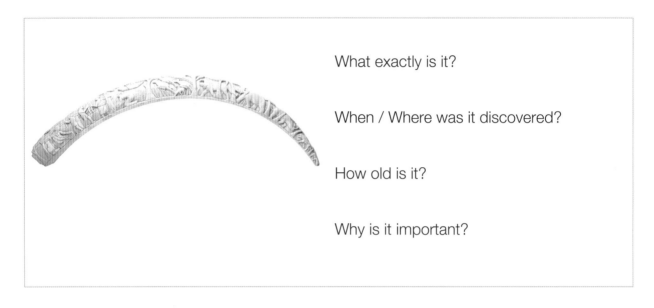

What exactly is it?

When / Where was it discovered?

How old is it?

Why is it important?

Unit 1.5 Exercise 2, page 18

STUDENT D

Marine iguana

Status
vulnerable
Why are numbers declining?
introduced predators, loss of nesting areas
Why do they need saving?
• They are the only iguanas that swim, so scientists have a lot to learn about them.
• Humans introduced their predators, so we have a responsibility to protect them.
Something to consider
Many tourists go to the Galápagos Islands to see them and other unique species.

Unit 2.5 Exercise 1, page 28

STUDENT D

Cindy is Rex's wife.
Max is Rex's son.
Mike is Max's uncle.
Susan is Max's sister.
Tom is Lucy's husband.
Alice is Lucy's daughter-in-law.
Ed is Carol's husband.
Cindy is Carol's granddaughter.

Unit 5.1 Exercise 10, page 53

A piece of furniture at the Milan International Furniture Fair

A sofa on display at the Museum of Decorative Arts, Paris

Unit 3.2 Exercise 7b, page 33

1 a reference book

2 Dickens

3 tsundoku

4 Sherlock Holmes

5 India

6 *Alice in Wonderland*

Audioscripts

Unit 1

▶ 1.2

My job, my passion, or what I'm trying to explore and share is the fact that we are throwing away the ark, which is my attempt to document as many of the world's captive species as I can before I die. I think photography has tremendous potential in terms of moving people to action.

These are pictures that go to work. These are pictures that work every day. Long after I'm dead, these things are going to go to work to save species. My goal is to get people to wake up and say, 'Whoa that's amazing! What do I gotta do to save that!?' And then they actually do save it.

To create a picture that outlasts us – that's really tough. I shoot 30,000 pictures a year, minimum. Maybe three or four are keepers. Three or four! I got more fingers on this hand than the numbers of keepers I get in a year, and all I do is shoot pictures, and that's all I've done since I was eighteen years old, is take pictures. But boy, those three or four are pretty good!

▶ 1.5

The barracuda is a species of fish that is doing pretty well and has a healthy population. The barracuda is classified as a species of least concern. The bigeye tuna, however, is not doing so well. Right now, there are certain things threatening the survival of the species – such as overfishing. As such, the bigeye tuna is classified as vulnerable. For vulnerable species like the bigeye tuna, it's important that we work to protect them now, before they become endangered or even extinct. The silver trout is just one example of a species of fish that is now extinct.

Unit 2

▶ 2.2

My family history is pretty interesting. I'm from Canada, but my ancestors all come from different places. My grandparents on my mother's side of the family moved from Scotland to Canada in the nineteenth century. In the 1930s though, my grandfather was working in England. So my mother, aunts and uncle were born in London and lived through World War Two. In the 1950s, my grandfather was offered a job in Canada, and so the family moved back there.

My grandfather on my father's side was from Transylvania, which is now part of Romania. In the 1920s, he went to university in Scotland. While he was there, he met, fell in love with and eventually married a local girl – my grandmother. They moved back to Transylvania, which is where my father was born. Shortly after though, they moved to neighbouring Hungary.

My father grew up in Hungary, but in 1956, there was a revolution and my father, who was nineteen at that time, was forced to leave. He eventually settled in Canada, which is where he met my mother. My father passed away in 2010, but our family is doing great. My mother and two brothers are still in Canada, my sister lives in Germany and I've been in Singapore since 2001. I'm still Canadian, but I'm proud of my Scottish and Hungarian background. And my wife is Singaporean, so that's made my family tree even more international.

▶ 2.6

A: Are you doing anything interesting this weekend?

B: Yes. I'm going to meet my second cousin, Chris.

A: Your second cousin?

B: Yeah, I'm researching my family tree. Chris is my grandfather's sister's grandchild. And he's bringing his daughter Emily, too. She's my second cousin once removed.

A: That's cool. How did you get in touch?

B: Through my grandfather. I'm going to ask Chris to help me find out more about the family. He seems really interested.

A: Where are you meeting them?

B: At my place. They can meet the rest of the family, too.

A: That's great.

Unit 3

▶ 3.2

I knew I wanted to be a writer from a very young age. I read a lot as a child, and I fell in love with imagining the lives of other people, the things they hope for and the experiences that change them. Empathy and imagination help a lot when you start to write stories of your own.

My first book was published in 2001, and it's called *Simple Recipes*. It's a collection of seven short stories, and revolves around family relationships – all the acts of trust or betrayal or love between parents and children, and between people whose lives are bound together.

One of the stories is about a Malaysian immigrant family who now live in Canada. The story is told from the perspective of the youngest child – a girl born in Canada after the family's arrival. She describes a misunderstanding between her father and brother – a result of the cultural, and also language, differences between the two generations that is an inescapable part of the immigrant experience.

Simple Recipes received a great deal of praise, which gave me the confidence to keep doing what I loved. Since then, I've published three more books. Writing stories and novels is an unusual way of life. Writing allows me to imagine and inhabit many different kinds of lives, and to expand the way I understand the world.

▶ 3.5

A: How many of these books have you read?

B: I've actually read them all except for *The Lion, the Witch and the Wardrobe*. Do you know it?

A: Yeah, it was one of my favourites when I was young.

B: What's it about?

A: Well, it's a children's story. It's about four brothers and sisters who live in an old house in England. They find an old wardrobe upstairs and it's magic.

B: How is it magic?

A: They can go through the wardrobe to visit a magical place called Narnia where they meet some talking animals.

B: Sounds interesting!

Unit 4

▶ 4.2

I = Iarla Ó Lionáird; N = narrator

I: My name is Iarla Ó Lionáird, and I'm an Irishman. I come from Cork – west Cork. And I'm a person who sings.

N: Ó Lionáird sings in a traditional style called sean-nós. He sings in Gaelic, which was Ó Lionáird's first language as a child. He was five years old before he learned English. Ó Lionáird was the eighth of twelve children. His mother and grandmother were also singers in the sean-nós style.

I: I remember my first day in school. Mrs McSweeney – Mrs Mac – was my teacher. I remember she lifted me up and she stood me on a desk, the first day I was ever in school, I was about five, and she said, 'sing'. It was almost as if there was shoes there waiting for me to put my feet into.

N: Ó Lionáird released his first of three solo albums in 1997. He is now a member of a group called The Gloaming. The group released its award-winning first album in 2014.

▶ 4.7

Many students listen to music when they study. Is this a good idea? Well, it depends on what they listen to. Songs without lyrics are generally OK, such as classical music. Songs with lyrics can distract you from studying, so it's best to avoid those. Some research also suggests that we study better when we listen to songs we like. Songs that we like help us to relax. Songs we dislike are going to annoy and distract us from our studies. So it may be best to listen to your favourite album rather than the radio.

Unit 5

▶ 5.2

I've been an interior designer now for about sixteen years. My mother and father were both architects so it was always likely that I'd have a career in design. I enjoyed art a lot in school, and I studied textile design when I was at university. I really learned a lot there, not just about textiles, but about design in general.

Every home I design is very different because every client is unique. I spend a lot of time talking with clients and learning about their personal needs and tastes. I want the finished space to reflect them as individuals, not myself as a designer.

There is a quote from a famous British designer called William Morris which I use as a starting point for every project. He said, 'Have nothing in your houses that you do not know to be useful or believe to be beautiful.' I think it's really helpful to think about interior design in terms of those two factors. Everything in your home should be either useful, or beautiful. If it isn't either, it shouldn't be there! And, in regard to ideas about what's beautiful, it's really important to respect and value your client's personal taste.

▶ 5.5

Let me explain to you a little more about three of the main features of a coat of arms. One of the first things people notice is the motto. It's a very common feature, but some coats of arms do not have it. This motto is in Latin. In English, it means, 'To be, rather than to seem'. The motto here is above the crest, but sometimes the motto appears below the shield.

The supporters are also a key element. Supporters are usually animals, but they can also be people. The two supporters can also be different – for example, in this coat of arms, you can see a unicorn and a lion. And then, of course, there's the shield. The design on the shield is very important. The different symbols that are used all have meaning. Even the shape of the shield – which can vary – carries some kind of meaning.

Unit 6

▶ 6.2

Narrator: Franklin Chang Díaz is an engineer, and a former NASA astronaut. As an astronaut, he went on seven Space Shuttle missions and was the third Latin-American to go into space. But what inspired him in his career?

Franklin Chang Díaz: I was a child of the fifties. I was captivated by space because of the launch of Sputnik. Sputnik was something that probably lit the fire or lit the spark of space for many children. I have many heroes. Still do. The number one hero is my dad. My dad was the one person that I wanted to be like. He was not a scientist, he was not an engineer, but he was an adventurer. He was a guy that was not afraid of anything, and I wanted to be like him. Even today, when I'm faced with a difficult problem, I have to make a decision, I always ask myself, 'What would my father do in this same situation?' and it helps me a lot to arrive at a decision. Inspiration is in many ways a bit of a chain. I was inspired by others, and maybe I was, or I am, an inspiration to some. And that is part of the way it should be. I feel that this was not part of my plan, to be an inspiration, but it is a responsibility that I have acquired, and I have to be true to it. I hope that those that come after me will inspire others as well, and so the chain will be unbroken.

▶ 6.6

There are a lot of inspirational people in the world, but when I think about who I really admire, two people come to mind. The first is Leonardo da Vinci. We know him as a painter, of course, but he was much more than that. He was good at so many things – inventing, engineering, music, maths, astronomy, literature. He had such an incredible mind.

Another person I admire is Mexican artist Frida Kahlo. I admire her because she was such a strong person. And her self-portraits are fascinating. There is one quote I remember. She once said, 'I paint myself because I am so often alone and because I am the subject I know best.'

Unit 7

▶ 7.4

One of the things I really love about cooking is that it's such a universal experience. Food is how the vast majority of us interact with our resources. I worked as a fisherman in Africa, off the coast of Essaouira, and the sardine fishermen were out there, and until this point, seafood had just been delivered as if by magic. But here, in this village, in this ages old tradition, here is men and women who are casting nets into the sea in hopes of catching dinner – not dollars.

Environmentalism, at its root, is a human concern. Environmentalism is so often thought of as this distant idea – this whale that we need to save in some distant ocean far away. But dinner is full contact environmentalism.

▶ 7.7

Interviewer: Thank you for talking to us. So, we know that today, people around the world are eating more meat than ever before. Do you think this trend will continue in the future?

Expert: Yes, I do. We can be pretty sure about this. First of all, the world's population is increasing. Every day, there are around 228,000 more people on the planet! So, by 2050, we think that the population of the world will increase by about 35 per cent. And, of course, the demand for meat will increase as the population increases. But also, in developing countries, people are becoming richer. By 2050, many more people will be able to buy meat regularly. We think there will be a 100 per cent increase in demand for meat from developing countries.

So when you take the two together – the global population growth and the increased demand from developing countries – it means that, in the next 30 years, there will be a huge rise in the number of people demanding meat. The big question is, however, will we be able to produce enough meat for the increased demand? In my opinion, it won't be easy.

▶ 7.10

1 It'll be hotter and drier in some places.
2 We'll need to save water.
3 Wet places will get wetter.
4 Some plants will grow well.
5 Will the weather change?
6 Yes, I'm sure it will.

Unit 8

▶ 8.1

I grew up in a place called Whitworth. It's a very small town in the north of England. Only about 8,000 people live there, so it's a very quiet place. You can go walking in the countryside, which is lovely, but other than that, there's not much to do.

When I was 21, I moved to Singapore, which was a huge change. Singapore is a bustling, modern, multicultural city – the exact opposite of Whitworth! Singapore was a great place to live. I met people from so many different backgrounds and I had a really great time. I lived in Singapore for nine years, and then in 2009, I moved to Sydney, Australia, which is where I live now. Sydney is a wonderful place. I feel like I have the best of both worlds here. I live in the suburbs in a quiet neighbourhood not too far from the city. There are a lot of parks near where I live, and it's a pretty peaceful place. But if I want a bit more excitement, I'm only a short drive from the city centre. There's so much to do in Sydney, I never get bored. I've got no plans to move again in the future. I'm really happy where I am now.

▶ 8.5

A: Hey, this in interesting. It says Monterrey, Mexico, is one of the happiest cities in the world. You grew up there, right?

B: Yeah, that's right.

A: So, what do you think? Was it a happy city?

B: Well, I loved living there. I used to love hanging out with my friends on the riverfront. I didn't have a car in those days, but it was so easy to get around by bus. I was always happy.

A: Cool. I should visit there one day.

B: Yeah. If you go, make sure you check out the Santa Lucia Riverwalk. It's really cool.

A: OK, thanks for the advice.

Unit 9

▶ 9.1

In 2016, I and a group of friends took part in an event called the Dumball Rally in India. The event was to raise money for a charity called the Teenage Cancer Trust. The rally involved about 30 teams. Each team had a car, which they drove around the southern part of India. The journey took eight days. We started in Chennai, we drove south along the east coast, and then north up the west coast, and finished in our final destination, in Goa.

We used social media to ask our friends and family for donations. Using Facebook and a website called JustGiving.com, it was really easy to contact everyone to receive their donations online. Our team raised around $4,000, and in total, the event raised around $170,000.

And of course, the journey itself was lots of fun, too. We drove for about twelve hours every day, and saw some incredible scenery along the way. We also got a chance to talk to some of the local people, and we even managed to have a game of cricket! It was an experience I will never forget, and hopefully the money we raised will go some way to making people's lives better.

▶ 9.6

A: I heard you're planning to run a marathon for charity.

B: Yeah, that's right. I'm raising money for a local children's charity.

A: That's great. Can I make a donation?

B: Of course. I have a Facebook page where you can donate online.

A: OK, cool. I'll do it later today. How much have you raised so far?

B: Well, so far it's $950. So, if you donate $50, I'll reach my target of $1,000.

A: Oh, well done! OK, $50 is no problem.

B: Great! Thanks.

Unit 10

▶ 10.1

The human brain is the most complex organ in the human body. There are five main parts.

The frontal lobe is the part of our brain that helps us concentrate. We use it when we are trying to solve problems. But it's also responsible for our emotions, and so it influences our personality quite a lot. The occipital lobe as at the back of the brain. It helps us understand things that we see, such as colour, shape and distance. It's also the part of our brain that makes us dream. The temporal lobe is the part responsible for our long-term memory. It helps us organize information and understand language. The cerebellum helps us balance and control our muscles. It's important for hand-eye coordination.

The parietal lobe is the part that is responsible for our pain and touch sensations. It also enables us to understand time, numbers, and to be able to spell words. The brain is a truly amazing thing, and there's still so much that we don't know about it.

▶ 10.2

How good would you say that your hand-eye coordination is? Good? Really good? Do you wish you could improve it? Many athletes believe that simply visualizing an action can improve their coordination. But does it work? Let's find out.

Let's run our experiment on the greatest sport ever invented. Set up a waste basket, crumple up some pieces of paper, and try to make some baskets. Sometimes you miss your shot. Sometimes you make it. Here's our question: can visualizing your throw before you take it improve your shooting?

This time, before shooting, try visualizing what it'll feel like for your arm to take the shot, and also the path that the paper will take on its way to the basket. Get set up. Do you see it? OK, then take the shot. If you're playing along at home, try taking a bunch of shots. On half of them, try visualizing first. On the other half, just go ahead and shoot. Keep track of your performance. Does it really help to visualize?

There's some evidence that mental practice of this sort can actually improve some types of athletic performance. Now some of these improvements might just be due to getting yourself into a relaxed and focused state of mind. But some of them might be because visualizing actions turns out to activate some of the same brain regions produced in making the motions themselves.

▶ 10.7

The brain is incredible, and scientists are learning more and more about it every day. Did you know, for example, that your brain is able to generate power? Experts believe that it can generate enough electricity to power a light bulb.

There are also some common myths about the brain. You may have heard that we only use ten per cent of our brains. Well, most scientists now agree that that's not true. We use different parts of our brains for different purposes at different times. So the percentage is generally higher.

And do men have bigger brains than women? It appears so, although not by much. Men's brains are on average about ten per cent larger than women's. When you think about it, it makes sense. Men's bodies are generally bigger than women's.

Unit 11

▶ 11.1

I love nature. I've always been a fan of nature. I'm now lucky enough that I live in a part of the world where I'm near a beach, and near a lovely park where I enjoy cycling. I sometimes see large monitor lizards and exotic birds, and I really enjoy it.

I've been on a couple of nature holidays. My last one was in Greece. It was a Greek island called Zakynthos, which is famous for turtles. We went in June, and we were lucky enough to see the baby turtles on the beach, and we took some wonderful photographs. I've also been to Cairns, which is in Australia, and we went snorkelling at the Great Barrier Reef, which was amazing. We saw nurse sharks, we saw jellyfish, we saw other colourful fish, and I even saw an octopus. I would really like to visit South Africa to go on safari, to see animals in the wild, in their natural habitat. I would love to take some photographs of the lions and the giraffes. I think that would be an amazing adventure.

▶ 11.6

Many children around the world are having less contact with nature. They spend more time indoors than ever before. They lack basic knowledge of nature. What can we do about this? First, we as adults need to set an example for our children. Adults need to connect with nature as well. Take your kids camping. Go for a walk. Play games together in the park. When you do fun things with your kids outside, they will want to spend more time there.

And second, I'd suggest we need to look at why children are staying indoors more. They watch TV. They play on computers and other electronic devices. My advice for parents is to set aside a few hours a week as 'Turn off time'. For these few hours, don't allow children to use electronic devices, and instead, encourage them to do something outside.

Unit 12

▶ 12.1

Narrator: In February 1982, archaeologist Fredrik Hiebert made an exciting discovery.

Fredrik Hiebert: One of the great stories that I have is about a time that I was excavating a trade site on the coast of Egypt. The site's more than 800 years old, and we were excavating a merchant's house who had been there seasonally, who had lived there in the summers when ships came, and then he would leave. And I was brushing the doorway, and I noticed there was a doormat. And I lifted up that doormat, and what was underneath that but a wooden key! That key was over 800 years old! And I picked it up and noticed that it had the name of the merchant written on it. Can you imagine? That merchant had been there 800 years ago, left his key, hoping to come back, and we found it. It was such a close connection with the past. It was awesome!

▶ 12.5

The terracotta warriors were discovered in 1974. Since then, millions of people have visited this incredible site in Xian, China. Scientists have learned a great deal about the terracotta warriors in the past few decades. The site is actually a tomb. It was built for the first emperor of China over 2,000 years ago.

The 8,000 or so sculptures are all different – no two are alike. When tourists look at them today, they see brown. But the soldiers were originally painted in bright colours. This was done to make them look more realistic. The colours have faded over time.

TED Talk transcripts

The transcripts use British English for all the talks, irrespective of the nationality of the speaker.

Any grammatical inaccuracies in the talks have been left uncorrected in the transcripts.

Unit 1 Munir Virani: Why I love vultures

Part 1

I would like to talk to you about a very special group of animals. There are 10,000 species of birds in the world. Vultures are amongst the most threatened group of birds. When you see a vulture like this, the first thing that comes to your mind is, these are disgusting, ugly, greedy creatures that are just after your flesh, associated with politicians. I want to change that perception. I want to change those feelings you have for these birds, because they need our sympathy. They really do. And I'll tell you why.

First of all, why do they have such a bad press? When Charles Darwin went across the Atlantic in 1832 on the Beagle, he saw the turkey vulture, and he said, 'These are disgusting birds with bald scarlet heads that are formed to revel in putridity.' You could not get a worse insult, and that from Charles Darwin. You know, he changed his mind when he came back, and I'll tell you why. They've also been associated with Disney – personified as goofy, dumb, stupid characters.

[…] So there's two types of vultures in this planet. There are the New World vultures that are mainly found in the Americas, like the condors and the caracaras, and then the Old World vultures, where we have sixteen species. From these sixteen, eleven of them are facing a high risk of extinction.

So why are vultures important? First of all, they provide vital ecological services. They clean up. They're our natural garbage collectors. They clean up carcasses right to the bone. They help to kill all the bacteria. They help absorb anthrax that would otherwise spread and cause huge livestock losses and diseases in other animals. Recent studies have shown that in areas where there are no vultures, carcasses take up to three to four times to decompose, and this has huge ramifications for the spread of diseases.

Part 2

So what is the problem with vultures? We have eight species of vultures that occur in Kenya, of which six are highly threatened with extinction. […] In South Asia, in countries like India and Pakistan, four species of vultures are listed as critically endangered, which means they have less than ten or fifteen years to go extinct.

[…] So what's being done? Well, we're conducting research on these birds. We're putting transmitters on them. We're trying to determine their basic ecology, and see where they go. We can see that they travel different countries, so if you focus on a problem locally, it's not going to help you. We need to work with governments in regional levels. We're working with local communities. We're talking to them about appreciating vultures, about the need from within to appreciate these wonderful creatures and the services that they provide.

How can you help? You can become active, make noise. You can write a letter to your government and tell them that we need to focus on these very misunderstood creatures. Volunteer your time to spread the word. Spread the word. When you walk out of this room, you will be informed about vultures, but speak to your families, to your children, to your neighbours about vultures.

They are very graceful. Charles Darwin said he changed his mind because he watched them fly effortlessly without energy in the skies. Kenya, this world, will be much poorer without these wonderful species. Thank you very much.

Unit 2 A. J. Jacobs: The world's largest family reunion

Part 1

Six months ago, I got an email from a man in Israel who had read one of my books, and the email said, 'You don't know me, but I'm your twelfth cousin.' And it said, 'I have a family tree with 80,000 people on it, including you, Karl Marx, and several European aristocrats.'

[…] So this email inspired me to dive into genealogy, which I always thought was a very staid and proper field, but it turns out it's going through a fascinating revolution, and a controversial one. Partly, this is because of DNA and genetic testing, but partly, it's because of the Internet. There are sites that now take the Wikipedia approach to family trees, collaboration and crowdsourcing, and what you do is, you load your family tree on, and then these sites search to see if the A. J. Jacobs in your tree is the same as the A. J. Jacobs in another tree, and if it is, then you can combine, and then you combine and combine and combine until you get these massive, mega-family trees with thousands of people on them, or even millions. I'm on something on Geni called the world family tree, which has no less than a jaw-dropping 75 million people. So that's 75 million people connected by blood or marriage, sometimes both. It's in all seven continents, including Antarctica. I'm on it. Many of you are on it, whether you know it or not, and you can see the links. Here's my cousin Gwyneth Paltrow. She has no idea I exist, but we are officially cousins. We have just seventeen links between us. And there's my cousin Barack Obama. And he is my aunt's fifth great-aunt's husband's father's wife's seventh great-nephew, so practically my older brother.

[…] Now, I'm not boasting, because all of you have famous people and historical figures in your tree, because we are all connected, and 75 million may seem like a lot, but in a few years, it's quite likely we will have a family tree with all, almost all, seven billion people on Earth. But does it really matter? What's the importance?

Part 2

First, it's got scientific value. This is an unprecedented history of the human race, and it's giving us valuable data about how diseases are inherited, how people migrate, and there's a team of scientists at MIT right now studying the world family tree.

Number two, it brings history alive. I found out I'm connected to Albert Einstein, so I told my seven-year-old son that, and he was totally engaged. Now Albert Einstein is not some dead white guy with weird hair. He's Uncle Albert.

[...] Number three, interconnectedness. We all come from the same ancestor, [...] so that means we literally all are biological cousins as well, and estimates vary, but probably the farthest cousin you have on Earth is about a 50th cousin. Now, it's not just ancestors we share, descendants. If you have kids, and they have kids, look how quickly the descendants accumulate. So in ten, twelve generations, you're going to have thousands of offspring, and millions of offspring.

Number four, a kinder world. Now, I know that there are family feuds. I have three sons, so I see how they fight. But I think that there's also a human bias to treat your family a little better than strangers. I think this tree is going to be bad news for bigots, because they're going to have to realize that they are cousins with thousands of people in whatever ethnic group they happen to have issues with, and I think you look back at history, and a lot of the terrible things we've done to each other is because one group thinks another group is sub-human, and you can't do that anymore. We're not just part of the same species. We're part of the same family. We share 99.9 per cent of our DNA.

Part 3

So I have all these hundreds and thousands, millions of new cousins. I thought, what can I do with this information? And that's when I decided, why not throw a party? So that's what I'm doing. And you're all invited. Next year, next summer, I will be hosting what I hope is the biggest and best family reunion in history. Thank you. I want you there. I want you there. It's going to be at the New York Hall of Science, which is a great venue,

[...] There's going to be exhibits and food, music. Paul McCartney is eleven steps away, so I'm hoping he brings his guitar. He hasn't RSVP'd yet, but fingers crossed. And there is going to be a day of speakers, of fascinating cousins.

[…] And, of course, the most important is that you, I want you guys there, and I invite you to go to GlobalFamilyReunion.org and figure out how you're on the family tree, because these are big issues, family and tribe, and I don't know all the answers, but I have a lot of smart relatives, including you guys, so together, I think we can figure it out. Only together can we solve these big problems. So from cousin to cousin, I thank you. I can't wait to see you. Goodbye.

Unit 3 Ann Morgan: My year reading a book from every country

Part 1

It's often said that you can tell a lot about a person by looking at what's on their bookshelves. What do my bookshelves say about me? Well, when I asked myself this question a few years ago, I made an alarming discovery. I'd always thought of myself as a fairly cultured, cosmopolitan sort of person. But my bookshelves told a rather different story. Pretty much all the titles on them were by British or North American authors, and there was almost nothing in translation. Discovering this massive, cultural blind spot in my reading came as quite a shock.

And when I thought about it, it seemed like a real shame. I knew there had to be lots of amazing stories out there

by writers working in languages other than English. And it seemed really sad to think that my reading habits meant I would probably never encounter them. So, I decided to prescribe myself an intensive course of global reading. 2012 was set to be a very international year for the UK; it was the year of the London Olympics. And so I decided to use it as my time frame to try and read a novel, short story collection or memoir from every country in the world. And so I did. And it was very exciting and I learned some remarkable things and made some wonderful connections that I want to share with you today.

Part 2

So how on earth was I going to read the world? I was going to have to ask for help. So in October 2011, I registered my blog, ayearofreadingtheworld.com, and I posted a short appeal online. I explained who I was, how narrow my reading had been, and I asked anyone who cared to to leave a message suggesting what I might read from other parts of the planet. Now, I had no idea whether anyone would be interested, but within a few hours of me posting that appeal online, people started to get in touch. At first, it was friends and colleagues. Then it was friends of friends. And pretty soon, it was strangers.

Four days after I put that appeal online, I got a message from a woman called Rafidah in Kuala Lumpur. She said she loved the sound of my project, could she go to her local English-language bookshop and choose my Malaysian book and post it to me? I accepted enthusiastically, and a few weeks later, a package arrived containing not one, but two books – Rafidah's choice from Malaysia, and a book from Singapore that she had also picked out for me. Now, at the time, I was amazed that a stranger more than 6,000 miles away would go to such lengths to help someone she would probably never meet.

But Rafidah's kindness proved to be the pattern for that year. Time and again, people went out of their way to help me. Some took on research on my behalf, and others made detours on holidays and business trips to go to bookshops for me. It turns out, if you want to read the world, if you want to encounter it with an open mind, the world will help you.

Part 3

The books I read that year opened my eyes to many things. As those who enjoy reading will know, books have an extraordinary power to take you out of yourself and into someone else's mindset, so that, for a while at least, you look at the world through different eyes. That can be an uncomfortable experience, particularly if you're reading a book from a culture that may have quite different values to your own. But it can also be really enlightening. Wrestling with unfamiliar ideas can help clarify your own thinking. And it can also show up blind spots in the way you might have been looking at the world.

When I looked back at much of the English-language literature I'd grown up with, for example, I began to see quite how narrow a lot of it was, compared to the richness that the world has to offer. And as the pages turned, something else started to happen, too. Little by little, that long list of countries that I'd started the year with, changed from a rather dry, academic register of place names into living, breathing entities.

Now, I don't want to suggest that it's at all possible to get a rounded picture of a country simply by reading one book. But cumulatively, the stories I read that year made me more alive than ever before to the richness, diversity and complexity of our remarkable planet. It was as though the world's stories and the people who'd gone to such lengths to help me read them had made it real to me. These days, when I look at my bookshelves or consider the works on my e-reader, they tell a rather different story. It's the story of the power books have to connect us across political, geographical, cultural, social, religious divides. It's the tale of the potential human beings have to work together.

[…] And I hope many more people will join me. If we all read more widely, there'd be more incentive for publishers to translate more books, and we would all be richer for that.

Thank you.

Unit 4 Daria van den Bercken: Why I take the piano on the road … and in the air

Part 1

Recently, I flew over a crowd of thousands of people in Brazil, playing music by George Frideric Handel. I also drove along the streets of Amsterdam, again playing music by this same composer. Let's take a look.

[Music: George Frideric Handel, 'Allegro'. Performed by Daria van den Bercken.]

[Video] Daria van den Bercken: I live there on the third floor. [In Dutch] I live there on the corner. I actually live there, around the corner … and you'd be really welcome.

Man: [In Dutch] Does that sound like fun?

Child: [In Dutch] Yes!

Daria van den Bercken: All this was a real magical experience for hundreds of reasons. Now you may ask, why have I done these things? They're not really typical for a musician's day-to-day life. Well, I did it because I fell in love with the music and I wanted to share it with as many people as possible.

It started a couple of years ago. I was sitting at home on the couch with the flu and browsing the Internet a little, when I found out that Handel had written works for the keyboard. Well, I was surprised. I did not know this. So I downloaded the sheet music and started playing. And what happened next was that I entered this state of pure, unprejudiced amazement. It was an experience of being totally in awe of the music, and I had not felt that in a long time. It might be easier to relate to this when you hear it. The first piece that I played through started like this. [Music] Well, this sounds very melancholic, doesn't it? And I turned the page and what came next was this. [Music] Well, this sounds very energetic, doesn't it? So within a couple of minutes, and the piece isn't even finished yet, I experienced two very contrasting characters: beautiful melancholy and sheer energy. And I consider these two elements to be vital human expressions. And the purity of the music makes you hear it very effectively.

Part 2

I've given a lot of children's concerts for children of seven and eight years old, and whatever I play, whether it's Bach, Beethoven, even Stockhausen, or some jazzy music, they are open to hear it, really willing to listen, and they are comfortable doing so. And when classes come in with children who are just a few years older, eleven, twelve, I felt that I sometimes already had trouble in reaching them like that. The complexity of the music does become an issue, and actually the opinions of others – parents, friends, media – they start to count. But the young ones, they don't question their own opinion. They are in this constant state of wonder, and I do firmly believe that we can keep listening like these seven-year-old children, even when growing up. And that is why I have played not only in the concert hall but also on the street, online, in the air: to feel that state of wonder, to truly listen, and to listen without prejudice. And I'd like to invite you to do so now. [music]

Thank you.

Unit 5 Roman Mars: The worst-designed thing you've never noticed

Part 1

I know what you're thinking: 'Why does that guy get to sit down?' That's because this is radio.

I tell radio stories about design, and I report on all kinds of stories: buildings and toothbrushes and mascots and wayfinding and fonts. My mission is to get people to engage with the design that they care about so they begin to pay attention to all forms of design.

[…] And few things give me greater joy than a well-designed flag. Yeah! Happy 50th anniversary on your flag, Canada. It is beautiful, gold standard. Love it. I'm kind of obsessed with flags. Sometimes I bring up the topic of flags, and people are like, 'I don't care about flags', and then we start talking about flags, and trust me, 100 per cent of people care about flags. There's just something about them that works on our emotions.

[...] OK. So when I moved back to San Francisco in 2008, I researched its flag, because I had never seen it in the previous eight years I lived there. And I found it, I am sorry to say, sadly lacking. I know. It hurts me, too.

Part 2

Narrator: The five basic principles of flag design. Number one. Ted Kaye: Keep it simple.

Narrator: Number two. TK: Use meaningful symbolism.

Narrator: Number three. TK: Use two to three basic colours.

Narrator: Number four. TK: No lettering or seals.

Narrator: Never use writing of any kind. TK: Because you can't read that at a distance.

Narrator: Number five. TK: And be distinctive.

Roman Mars: All the best flags tend to stick to these principles. And like I said before, most country flags are OK. But here's the thing: if you showed this list of principles to any designer of almost anything, they would say these principles – simplicity, deep meaning, having few colours or being thoughtful about colours, uniqueness, don't have writing you can't read – all those principles apply to them, too.

[...] But here's the trick: if you want to design a great flag, a kickass flag like Chicago's or DC's, which also has a great flag, start by drawing a one-by-one-and-a-half-inch rectangle on a piece of paper. Your design has to fit within that tiny rectangle. Here's why.

TK: A three-by-five-foot flag on a pole 100 feet away looks about the same size as a one-by-one-and-a-half-inch rectangle seen about 15 inches from your eye. You'd be surprised at how compelling and simple the design can be when you hold yourself to that limitation.

RM: Meanwhile, back in San Francisco. Is there anything we can do?

TK: I like to say that in every bad flag there's a good flag trying to get out. The way to make San Francisco's flag a good flag is to take the motto off because you can't read that at a distance. Take the name off, and the border might even be made thicker, so it's more a part of the flag. And I would simply take the phoenix and make it a great big element in the middle of the flag.

RM: But the current phoenix, that's got to go.

TK: I would simplify or stylize the phoenix. Depict a big, wide-winged bird coming out of flames. Emphasize those flames.

RM: So this San Francisco flag was designed by Frank Chimero based on Ted Kaye's suggestions. I don't know what he would do if he was completely unfettered and didn't follow those guidelines. Fans of my radio show and podcast, they've heard me complain about bad flags. They've sent me other suggested designs. This one's by Neil Mussett. Both are so much better. And I think if they were adopted, I would see them around the city.

Part 3

TK: Often when city leaders say, 'We have more important things to do than worry about a city flag', my response is, 'If you had a great city flag, you would have a banner for people to rally under to face those more important things.'

[...] So maybe all the city flags can be as inspiring as Hong Kong or Portland or Trondheim, and we can do away with all the bad flags like San Francisco, Milwaukee, Cedar Rapids, and finally, when we're all done, we can do something about Pocatello, Idaho, considered by the North American Vexillological Association as the worst city flag in North America. Yeah. That thing has a trademark symbol on it, people. That hurts me just to look at. Thank you so much for listening.

Unit 6 Jarrett J. Krosoczka: How a boy became an artist

Part 1

When I was in the third grade, a monumental event happened. An author visited our school, Jack Gantos. A published author of books came to talk to us about what he did for a living. And afterwards, we all went back to our classrooms and we drew our own renditions of his main character, Rotten Ralph. And suddenly the author appeared in our doorway, and I remember him sort of sauntering down the aisles, going from kid to kid looking at the desks, not saying a word. But he stopped next to my desk, and he tapped on my desk, and he said, 'Nice cat'. And he wandered away. Two words that made a colossal difference in my life. When I was in the third grade, I wrote a book for the first time, 'The Owl Who Thought He Was The Best Flyer'.

[...] So I loved writing so much that I'd come home from school, and I would take out pieces of paper, and I would

staple them together, and I would fill those blank pages with words and pictures just because I loved using my imagination. And so these characters would become my friends. There was an egg, a tomato, a head of lettuce and a pumpkin, and they all lived in this refrigerator city, and in one of their adventures they went to a haunted house that was filled with so many dangers, like an evil blender who tried to chop them up, an evil toaster who tried to kidnap the bread couple, and an evil microwave who tried to melt their friend who was a stick of butter.

Part 2

So how did I make friends? I drew funny pictures of my teachers – and I passed them around. Well, in English class, in ninth grade, my friend John, who was sitting next to me, laughed a little bit too hard. Mr Greenwood was not pleased. He instantly saw that I was the cause of the commotion, and for the first time in my life, I was sent to the hall, and I thought, 'Oh no, I'm doomed. My grandfather's just going to kill me.' And he came out to the hallway and he said, 'Let me see the paper.' And I thought, 'Oh no. He thinks it's a note.' And so I took this picture, and I handed it to him. And we sat in silence for that brief moment, and he said to me, 'You're really talented. You're really good. You know, the school newspaper needs a new cartoonist, and you should be the cartoonist. Just stop drawing in my class.' So my parents never found out about it. I didn't get in trouble.

[...] I kept making comics, and at the Worcester Art Museum, I was given the greatest piece of advice by any educator I was ever given. Mark Lynch, he's an amazing teacher and he's still a dear friend of mine, and I was fourteen or fifteen, and I walked into his comic book class halfway through the course, and I was so excited, I was beaming. I had this book that was how to draw comics in the Marvel way, and it taught me how to draw superheroes, how to draw a woman, how to draw muscles just the way they were supposed to be if I were to ever draw for X-Men or Spider-Man. And all the colour just drained from his face, and he looked at me, and he said, 'Forget everything you learned.' And I didn't understand. He said, 'You have a great style. Celebrate your own style. Don't draw the way you're being told to draw. Draw the way you're drawing and keep at it, because you're really good.'

Part 3

I graduated from RISD. My grandparents were very proud, and I moved to Boston, and I set up shop. I set up a studio and I tried to get published. I would send out my books. I would send out hundreds of postcards to editors and art directors, but they would go unanswered.

[...] Now, I used to work the weekends at the Hole in the Wall off-season programming to make some extra money as I was trying to get my feet off the ground, and this kid who was just this really hyper kid, I started calling him 'Monkey Boy', and I went home and wrote a book called 'Good Night, Monkey Boy'. And I sent out one last batch of postcards. And I received an email from an editor at Random House with a subject line, 'Nice work!' Exclamation point. 'Dear Jarrett, I received your postcard. I liked your art, so I went to your website and I'm wondering if you ever tried writing any of your own stories, because I really like your art and it looks like there are some stories that go with them. Please let me know if you're ever in New York City.' And this was from an editor at Random House Children's Books. So the next week I 'happened' to be in New York. And I met with this editor, and I left New York for a contract for my first book, 'Good Night, Monkey Boy', which was published on June 12, 2001.

[...] And then something happened that changed my life. I got my first piece of significant fan mail, where this kid loved Monkey Boy so much that he wanted to have a Monkey Boy birthday cake. For a two-year-old, that is like a tattoo. You know? You only get one birthday per year. And for him, it's only his second. And I got this picture, and I thought, 'This picture is going to live within his consciousness for his entire life. He will forever have this photo in his family photo albums.' So that photo, since that moment, is framed in front of me while I've worked on all of my books.

[...] And I get the most amazing fan mail, and I get the most amazing projects, and the biggest moment for me came last Halloween. The doorbell rang and it was a trick-or-treater dressed as my character. It was so cool.

Unit 7 Andras Forgacs: Leather and meat without killing animals

Part 1

I'm convinced that in 30 years, when we look back on today and on how we raise and slaughter billions of animals to make our hamburgers and our handbags, we'll see this as being wasteful and indeed crazy. Did you know that today we maintain a global herd of 60 billion animals to provide our meat, dairy, eggs and leather goods? And over the next few decades, as the world's population expands to ten billion, this will need to nearly double to 100 billion animals.

But maintaining this herd takes a major toll on our planet. Animals are not just raw materials. They're living beings, and already our livestock is one of the largest users of land, fresh water, and one of the biggest producers of greenhouse gases, which drive climate change. On top of this, when you get so many animals so close together, it creates a breeding ground for disease and opportunities for harm and abuse. Clearly, we cannot continue on this path which puts the environment, public health and food security at risk. There is another way, . . .

Part 2

There is another way, because essentially, animal products are just collections of tissues, and right now we breed and raise highly complex animals only to create products that are made of relatively simple tissues. What if, instead of starting with a complex and sentient animal, we started with what the tissues are made of, the basic unit of life, the cell? This is biofabrication, where cells themselves can be used to grow biological products like tissues and organs.

[...] And we should begin by reimagining leather. I emphasize leather because it is so widely used. It is beautiful, and it has long been a part of our history. Growing leather is also technically simpler than growing other animal products like meat. It mainly uses one cell type, and it is largely two-dimensional.

Part 3

And so I'm very excited to show you, for the first time, the first batch of our cultured leather, fresh from the lab. This is real, genuine leather, without the animal sacrifice. It can have all the characteristics of leather because it is made of the same cells, and better yet, there is no hair to remove, no scars or insect's bites, and no waste. This leather can be grown in the shape of a wallet, a handbag or a car seat. It is not limited to the irregular shape of a cow or an alligator.

And because we make this material, we grow this leather from the ground up, we can control its properties in very interesting ways. This piece of leather is a mere seven tissue layers thick, and as you can see, it is nearly transparent. And this leather is 21 layers thick and quite opaque. You don't have that kind of fine control with conventional leather.

[...] We can design new materials, new products and new facilities. We need to move past just killing animals as a resource to something more civilized and evolved. Perhaps we are ready for something literally and figuratively more cultured. Thank you.

Unit 8 Alessandra Orofino: It's our city. Let's fix it

Part 1

Fifty-four per cent of the world's population lives in our cities. In developing countries, one third of that population is living in slums. Seventy-five per cent of global energy consumption occurs in our cities, and 80 per cent of gas emissions that cause global warming come from our cities. So things that you and I might think about as global problems, like climate change, the energy crisis or poverty, are really, in many ways, city problems. They will not be solved unless people who live in cities, like most of us, actually start doing a better job, because right now, we are not doing a very good one.

[...] Three years ago, I co-founded an organization called Meu Rio, and we make it easier for people in the city of Rio to organize around causes and places that they care about in their own city, and have an impact on those causes and places every day. In these past three years, Meu Rio grew to a network of 160,000 citizens of Rio. About 40 per cent of those members are young people aged 20 to 29. That is one in every fifteen young people of that age in Rio today.

Part 2

Amongst our members is this adorable little girl, Bia, to your right, and Bia was just eleven years old when she started a campaign using one of our tools to save her model public school from demolition. Her school actually ranks amongst the best public schools in the country, and it was going to be demolished by the Rio de Janeiro state government to build, I kid you not, a parking lot for the World Cup right before the event happened. Bia started a campaign, and we even watched her school 24/7 through webcam monitoring, and many months afterwards, the government changed their minds. Bia's school stayed in place.

There's also Jovita. She's an amazing woman whose daughter went missing about ten years ago, and since then, she has been looking for her daughter. In that process, she found out that first, she was not alone. In the last year alone, 2013, 6,000 people disappeared in the state of Rio. But she also found out that in spite of that, Rio had no centralized intelligence system for solving missing persons cases. In other Brazilian cities, those systems have helped solve up to 80 per cent of missing persons cases. She started a campaign, and after the secretary of security got 16,000 emails from people asking him to do this, he responded, and started to build a police unit specializing in those cases. It was open to the public at the end of last month, and Jovita was there giving interviews and being very fancy.

And then, there is Leandro. Leandro is an amazing guy in a slum in Rio, and he created a recycling project in the slum. At the end of last year, December 16, he received an eviction order by the Rio de Janeiro state government giving him two weeks to leave the space that he had been using for two years. The plan was to hand it over to a developer, who planned to turn it into a construction site. Leandro started a campaign using one of our tools, the Pressure Cooker, the same one that Bia and Jovita used, and the state government changed their minds before Christmas Eve.

Part 3

These stories make me happy, but not just because they have happy endings. They make me happy because they are happy beginnings. The teacher and parent community at Bia's school is looking for other ways they could improve that space even further. Leandro has ambitious plans to take his model to other low-income communities in Rio, and Jovita is volunteering at the police unit that she helped create.

[…] With the Our Cities network, the Meu Rio team hopes to share what we have learned with other people who want to create similar initiatives in their own cities. We have already started doing it in São Paulo with incredible results, and want to take it to cities around the world through a network of citizen-centric, citizen-led organizations that can inspire us, challenge us, and remind us to demand real participation in our city lives.

It is up to us to decide whether we want schools or parking lots, community-driven recycling projects or construction sites, loneliness or solidarity, cars or buses, and it is our responsibility to do that now, for ourselves, for our families, for the people who make our lives worth living, and for the incredible creativity, beauty, and wonder that make our cities, in spite of all of their problems, the greatest invention of our time. Obrigado. Thank you.

Unit 9 Joy Sun: Should you donate differently?

Part 1

I suspect that every aid worker in Africa comes to a time in her career when she wants to take all the money for her project – maybe it's a school or a training programme – pack it in a suitcase, get on a plane flying over the poorest villages in the country, and start throwing that money out the window. Because to a veteran aid worker, the idea of putting cold, hard cash into the hands of the poorest people on Earth doesn't sound crazy, it sounds really satisfying.

[…] Well, why did I spend a decade doing other stuff for the poor? Honestly, I believed that I could do more good with money for the poor than the poor could do for

themselves. I held two assumptions: one, that poor people are poor in part because they're uneducated and don't make good choices; two is that we then need people like me to figure out what they need and get it to them. It turns out, the evidence says otherwise.

Part 2

In recent years, researchers have been studying what happens when we give poor people cash. Dozens of studies show across the board that people use cash transfers to improve their own lives. Pregnant women in Uruguay buy better food and give birth to healthier babies. Sri Lankan men invest in their businesses. Researchers who studied our work in Kenya found that people invested in a range of assets, from livestock to equipment to home improvements, and they saw increases in income from business and farming one year after the cash was sent.

Part 3

One very telling study looked at a programme in India that gives livestock to the so-called ultra-poor, and they found that 30 per cent of recipients had turned around and sold the livestock they had been given for cash. The real irony is, for every 100 dollars' worth of assets this programme gave someone, they spent another 99 dollars to do it. What if, instead, we use technology to put cash, whether from aid agencies or from any one of us directly into a poor person's hands?

Part 4

Today, three in four Kenyans use mobile money, which is basically a bank account that can run on any cell phone. A sender can pay a 1.6 per cent fee and with the click of a button send money directly to a recipient's account with no intermediaries.

[…] That's what we've started to do at GiveDirectly. We're the first organization dedicated to providing cash transfers to the poor. We've sent cash to 35,000 people across rural Kenya and Uganda in one-time payments of 1,000 dollars per family. So far, we've looked for the poorest people in the poorest villages, and in this part of the world, they're the ones living in homes made of mud and thatch, not cement and iron.

[…] Something that five years ago would have seemed impossible we can now do efficiently and free of corruption. The more cash we give to the poor, and the more evidence we have that it works, the more we have to reconsider everything else we give. Today, the logic behind aid is too often, well, we do at least some good.

[…] What if the logic was, will we do better than cash given directly? Organizations would have to prove that they're doing more good for the poor than the poor can do for themselves. Of course, giving cash won't create public goods like eradicating disease or building strong institutions, but it could set a higher bar for how we help individual families improve their lives.

Unit 10 Tan Le: A headset that reads your brainwaves

Part 1

Up until now, our communication with machines has always been limited to conscious and direct forms. Whether it's something simple like turning on the lights with a switch, or even as complex as programming robotics, we have always had to give a command to a machine, or even a series of commands, in order for it to do something for us. Communication between people, on the other hand, is far more complex and a lot more interesting because we take into account so much more than what is explicitly expressed. We observe facial expressions, body language, and we can intuit feelings and emotions from our dialogue with one another. This actually forms a large part of our decision-making process. Our vision is to introduce this whole new realm of human interaction into human–computer interaction so that computers can understand not only what you direct it to do, but it can also respond to your facial expressions and emotional experiences. And what better way to do this than by interpreting the signals naturally produced by our brain, our centre for control and experience.

Part 2

So with that, I'd like to invite onstage Evan Grant, who is one of last year's speakers, who's kindly agreed to help me to demonstrate what we've been able to develop.

[…] So Evan, choose something that you can visualize clearly in your mind.

Evan Grant: Let's do 'pull'.

Tan Le: OK, so let's choose 'pull'. So the idea here now is that Evan needs to imagine the object coming forward into the screen, and there's a progress bar that will scroll across the screen while he's doing that. The first time, nothing will happen, because the system has no idea how he thinks about 'pull'. But maintain that thought for the entire duration of the eight seconds. So: one, two, three, go. OK. So once we accept this, the cube is live. So let's see if Evan can actually try and imagine pulling. Ah, good job! That's really amazing.

Part 3

So I'd like to show you a few examples, because there are many possible applications for this new interface. In games and virtual worlds, for example, your facial expressions can naturally and intuitively be used to control an avatar or virtual character. Obviously, you can experience the fantasy of magic and control the world with your mind. And also, colours, lighting, sound and effects can dynamically respond to your emotional state to heighten the experience that you're having, in real time. And moving on to some applications developed by developers and researchers around the world, with robots and simple machines, for example – in this case, flying a toy helicopter simply by thinking 'lift' with your mind.

The technology can also be applied to real world applications – in this example, a smart home. You know, from the user interface of the control system to opening curtains or closing curtains. And of course, also to the lighting – turning them on or off. And finally, to real life-changing applications, such as being able to control an electric wheelchair. In this example, facial expressions are mapped to the movement commands.

[Video] Man: Now blink right to go right. Now blink left to turn back left. Now smile to go straight.

TL: We really – thank you. We are really only scratching the surface of what is possible today, and with the community's input, and also with the involvement of developers and researchers from around the world, we hope that you can help us to shape where the technology goes from here. Thank you so much.

Unit 11 Louie Schwartzberg: The hidden beauty of pollination

Part 1

It's great being here at TED. You know, I think there might be some presentations that will go over my head, but the most amazing concepts are the ones that go right under my feet. The little things in life, sometimes that we forget about, like pollination, that we take for granted. And you can't tell the story about pollinators – bees, bats, hummingbirds, butterflies – without telling the story about the invention of flowers and how they co-evolved over 50 million years.

I've been filming time-lapse flowers 24 hours a day, seven days a week, for over 35 years. To watch them move is a dance I'm never going to get tired of. It fills me with wonder, and it opens my heart. Beauty and seduction, I believe, is nature's tool for survival, because we will protect what we fall in love with. Their relationship is a love story that feeds the Earth. It reminds us that we are a part of nature, and we're not separate from it.

When I heard about the vanishing bees, Colony Collapse Disorder, it motivated me to take action. We depend on pollinators for over a third of the fruits and vegetables we eat. And many scientists believe it's the most serious issue facing mankind. It's like the canary in the coalmine. If they disappear, so do we. It reminds us that we are a part of nature and we need to take care of it.

Part 2

Because I realized that nature had invented reproduction as a mechanism for life to move forward, as a life force that passes right through us and makes us a link in the evolution of life. Rarely seen by the naked eye, this intersection between the animal world and the plant world is truly a magic moment. It's the mystical moment where life regenerates itself, over and over again.

So here is some nectar from my film. I hope you'll drink, tweet and plant some seeds to pollinate a friendly garden. And always take time to smell the flowers, and let it fill you with beauty, and rediscover that sense of wonder. Here are some images from the film. [Music]

Thank you. Thank you very much. Thank you.

Unit 12 Nizar Ibrahim: How we unearthed the Spinosaurus

Part 1

These dragons from deep time are incredible creatures. They're bizarre, they're beautiful, and there's very little we know about them. These thoughts were going through my head when I looked at the pages of my first dinosaur book. I was about five years old at the time, and I decided there and then that I would become a palaeontologist. Palaeontology allowed me to combine my love for animals with my desire to travel to far-flung corners of the world.

And now, a few years later, I've led several expeditions to the ultimate far-flung corner on this planet, the Sahara.

I've worked in the Sahara because I've been on a quest to uncover new remains of a bizarre, giant predatory dinosaur called Spinosaurus.

A few bones of this animal have been found in the deserts of Egypt and were described about 100 years ago by a German palaeontologist. Unfortunately, all his Spinosaurus bones were destroyed in World War Two. So all we're left with are just a few drawings and notes. From these drawings, we know that this creature, which lived about 100 million years ago, was very big, it had tall spines on its back, forming a magnificent sail, and it had long, slender jaws, a bit like a crocodile, with conical teeth, that may have been used to catch slippery prey, like fish. But that was pretty much all we knew about this animal for the next 100 years.

Part 2

Finally, very recently, we were able to track down a dig site where a local fossil hunter found several bones of Spinosaurus. We returned to the site, we collected more bones. And so after 100 years we finally had another partial skeleton of this bizarre creature. And we were able to reconstruct it.

We now know that Spinosaurus had a head a little bit like a crocodile, very different from other predatory dinosaurs, very different from the T. rex. But the really interesting information came from the rest of the skeleton. We had long spines, the spines forming the big sail. We had leg bones, we had skull bones, we had paddle-shaped feet, wide feet – again, very unusual, no other dinosaur has feet like this – and we think they may have been used to walk on soft sediment, or maybe for paddling in the water. We also looked at the fine microstructure of the bone, the inside structure of Spinosaurus bones, and it turns out that they're very dense and compact. Again, this is something we see in animals that spend a lot of time in the water, it's useful for buoyancy control in the water.

We CT-scanned all of our bones and built a digital Spinosaurus skeleton. And when we looked at the digital skeleton, we realized that yes, this was a dinosaur unlike any other. It's bigger than a T. rex, and yes, the head has 'fish-eating' written all over it, but really the entire skeleton has 'water-loving' written all over it – dense bone, paddle-like feet, and the hind limbs are reduced in size, and again, this is something we see in animals that spend a substantial amount of time in the water.

Part 3

So, as we fleshed out our Spinosaurus – I'm looking at muscle attachments and wrapping our dinosaur in skin – we realize that we're dealing with a river monster, a predatory dinosaur, bigger than T. rex, the ruler of this ancient river of giants, feeding on the many aquatic animals I showed you earlier on.

So that's really what makes this an incredible discovery. It's a dinosaur like no other. And some people told me, 'Wow, this is a once-in-a-lifetime discovery. There are not many things left to discover in the world.' Well, I think nothing could be further from the truth. I think the Sahara's still full of treasures, and when people tell me there are no places left to explore, I like to quote a famous dinosaur hunter, Roy Chapman Andrews, and he said, 'Always, there has been an adventure just around the corner –

and the world is still full of corners.' That was true many decades ago when Roy Chapman Andrews wrote these lines. And it is still true today.

Thank you.

Irregular verb list

Infinitive	Past simple	Past participle	Translation	Infinitive	Past simple	Past participle	Translation
be	was / were	been		lend	lent	lent	
beat	beat	beaten		let	let	let	
become	became	become		lie	lay	lain	
begin	began	begun		light	lit	lit	
bend	bent	bent		lose	lost	lost	
bite	bit	bitten		make	made	made	
blow	blew	blown		mean /miːn/	meant /ment/	meant /ment/	
break	broke	broken		meet	met	met	
bring	brought	brought		must	had to	had to	
build	built	built		pay	paid	paid	
burn	burnt / burned	burnt / burned		put	put	put	
burst	burst	burst		read /riːd/	read /red/	read /red/	
can	could	been able to		ride	rode	ridden	
catch	caught	caught		ring	rang	rung	
choose	chose	chosen		rise	rose	risen	
come	came	come		run	ran	run	
cost	cost	cost		see	saw	seen	
cut	cut	cut		sell	sold	sold	
do	did	done		send	sent	sent	
draw	drew	drawn		set	set	set	
drive	drove	driven		shake	shook	shaken	
eat	ate	eaten		shine	shone	shone	
fall	fell	fallen		show	showed	shown	
feed	fed	fed		shut	shut	shut	
feel	felt	felt		sing	sang	sung	
fight	fought	fought		sink	sank	sunk	
find	found	found		sit	sat	sat	
fly	flew	flown		sleep	slept	slept	
forget	forgot	forgotten		spell	spelt / spelled	spelt / spelled	
forgive	forgave	forgiven		spend	spent	spent	
freeze	froze	frozen		stand	stood	stood	
give	gave	given		steal	stole	stolen	
go	went	gone		stick	stuck	stuck	
grow	grew	grown		swear	swore	sworn	
have	had	had		swim	swam	swum	
hear /ˈhɪə/	heard /hɜːd/	heard /hɜːd/		take	took	taken	
hide	hid	hidden		teach	taught	taught	
hit	hit	hit		tear	tore	torn	
hold	held	held		think	thought	thought	
hurt	hurt	hurt		throw	threw	thrown	
keep	kept	kept		understand	understood	understood	
know	knew	known		wake	woke	woken	
lay	laid	laid		wear	wore	worn	
lead	led	led		win	won	won	
leave	left	left					

Pre-intermediate Student's Book
David Bohlke with Stephanie Parker

Vice President, Editorial Director:
John McHugh

Executive Editor: Sian Mavor

Publishing Consultant: Karen Spiller

Development Editor: Sarah Ratcliff

Editorial Manager: Claire Merchant

Head of Strategic Marketing ELT:
Charlotte Ellis

Media Researcher: Leila Hishmeh

Senior Content Project Manager:
Nick Ventullo

Manufacturing Manager: Eyvett Davis

Cover/Text Design: Brenda Carmichael

Compositor: MPS North America LLC

Audio: Tom Dick and Debbie Productions Ltd

DVD: Tom Dick and Debbie Productions Ltd

Cover Photo: Siyanda Mohutsiwa speaks at
TED2016 - Dream, February 15–19, 2016,
Vancouver Convention Center, Vancouver,
Canada. © Bret Hartman/TED

For product information and technology assistance, contact us at
Cengage Learning Customer & Sales Support, cengage.com/contact

For permission to use material from this text or product,
submit all requests online at **cengage.com/permissions**
Further permissions questions can be emailed to
permissionrequest@cengage.com

Student's Book ISBN: 978-1-337-27392-3

National Geographic Learning
Cheriton House, North Way, Andover,
Hampshire, SP10 5BE
United Kingdom

National Geographic Learning, a Cengage Learning Company, has a mission to bring the world to the classroom and the classroom to life. With our English language programs, students learn about their world by experiencing it. Through our partnerships with National Geographic and TED Talks, they develop the language and skills they need to be successful global citizens and leaders.

Locate your local office at **international.cengage.com/region**

Visit National Geographic Learning online at **NGL.Cengage.com/ELT**
Visit our corporate website at **www.cengage.com**

Printed in Greece by Bakis SA
Print Number: 02   Print Year: 2017

CREDITS

The Author and Publisher would like to thank the following teaching professionals for their valuable input during the development of this series:

Coleeta Paradise Abdullah, Certified Training Center; Tara Amelia Arntsen, Northern State University; Estela Campos; Federica Castro, Pontificia Universidad Católica Madre y Maestra; Amy Cook, Bowling Green State University; Carrie Cheng, School of Continuing and Professional Studies, the University of Hong Kong; Mei-ho Chiu, Soochow University; Anthony Sean D'Amico, SDH Institute; Wilder Yesid Escobar Almeciga, Universidad El Bosque; Rosa E. Vasquez Fernandez, English for International Communication; Touria Ghaffari, The Beekman School; Rosario Giraldez, Alianza Cultural Uruguay Estados Unidos; William Haselton, NC State University; Yu Huichun, Macau University of Science and Technology; Michelle Kim, TOPIA Education; Jay Klaphake, Kyoto University of Foreign Studies; Kazuteru Kuramoto, Keio Senior High School; Michael McCollister, Feng Chia University; Jennifer Meldrum, EC English Language Centers; Holly Milkowart, Johnson County Community College; Nicholas Millward, Australian Centre for Education; Stella Maris Palavecino, Buenos Aires English House; Youngsun Park, YBM; Adam Parmentier, Mingdao High School; Jennie Popp, Universidad Andrés Bello; Terri Rapoport, ELS Educational Services; Erich Rose, Auburn University; Yoko Sakurai, Aichi University; Mark D. Sheehan, Hannan University; DongJin Shin, Hankuk University of Foreign Studies; Shizuka Tabara, Kobe University; Jeffrey Taschner, AUA Language Center; Hadrien Tournier, Berlitz Corporation; Rosa Vasquez, JFK Institute; Jindarat De Vleeschauwer, Chiang Mai University; Tamami Wada, Chubu University; Colin Walker, Myongii University; Elizabeth Yoon, Hanyang University; Keiko Yoshida, Konan University

And special thanks to: Tony Gainsford, Neil Glover, Fredrik Hiebert, Mary Kadera, Sarah Lafferty, Ken Lejtenyi, Joel Sartore, Barton Seaver, Claire Street, Madeleine Thien